# Armies of the Roman Republic 264–30 BC

# Armies of the Roman Republic 264–30 BC

## History, Organization and Equipment

Gabriele Esposito

Pen & Sword
MILITARY

First published in Great Britain in 2023 by
Pen & Sword Military
An imprint of Pen & Sword Books Limited
Yorkshire – Philadelphia



ISBN 978 1 39909 402 3



A CIP catalogue record for this book is
available from the British Library



Typeset in Adobe Caslon
by Mac Style

Printed and bound in India by Replika Press Pvt. Ltd.

MIX
Paper from
responsible sources
FSC® C016779
FSC
www.fsc.org

Pen & Sword Books Limited incorporates the imprints of After the Battle,
Atlas, Archaeology, Aviation, Discovery, Family History, Fiction, History,
Maritime, Military, Military Classics, Politics, Select, Transport, True Crime,
Air World, Frontline Publishing, Leo Cooper, Remember When, Seaforth
Publishing, The Praetorian Press, Wharncliffe Local History, Wharncliffe
Transport, Wharncliffe True Crime and White Owl.

For a complete list of Pen & Sword titles please contact

PEN & SWORD BOOKS LIMITED
47 Church Street, Barnsley, South Yorkshire, S70 2AS, England
E-mail: enquiries@pen-and-sword.co.uk
Website: www.pen-and-sword.co.uk
or
PEN AND SWORD BOOKS
1950 Lawrence Rd, Havertown, PA 19083, USA
E-mail: Uspen-and-sword@casematepublishers.com
Website: www.penandswordbooks.com

# Contents

Gabriele Esposito is a military historian who works as a freelance author and researcher for some of the most important publishing houses in the military history sector. In particular, he is an expert specializing in uniformology: his interests and expertise range from the ancient civilizations to modern post-colonial conflicts. During recent years, he has conducted and published several researches on the military history of the Latin American countries, with special attention on the War of the Triple Alliance and the War of the Pacific. He is among the leading experts on the military history of the Italian Wars of Unification and the Spanish Carlist Wars. His books and essays are published on a regular basis by Osprey Publishing, Winged Hussar Publishing and Libreria Editrice Goriziana; he is also the author of numerous military history articles appearing in specialized magazines like *Ancient Warfare Magazine*, *Medieval Warfare Magazine*, *The Armourer*, *History of War*, *Guerres et Histoire*, *Focus Storia* and *Focus Storia Wars*.

# Acknowledgements

This book is dedicated to my magnificent parents, Maria Rosaria and Benedetto, for the immense love and fundamental support that they have always given me. Their precious advice over many years has been instrumental in the creation of the book. A very special thanks goes to Philip Sidnell, the commissioning editor of my books for Pen & Sword: his love for history and his passion for publishing are the key factors behind the success of our publications. Many thanks also to the production manager of this title, Matt Jones, for his excellent work and immense enthusiasm. Special thanks are due to Tony Walton for editing my original manuscript using his great skill and knowledge. A very special mention also goes to the brilliant re-enactment groups that collaborated with their photographs in the creation of this book: without the incredible research work by their members, the final result of this publication would not have been the same. Consequently, I want to express my deep gratitude to the following living history associations: Aera Legio I Consularis from Provence (especially Jean-Luc Féraud), Ala I Batavorum from the Netherlands (particularly Jurjen Draaisma), Divulgación Histórica TANIT from Spain (especially Diego Casillas), Legio II Traiana Fortis – Cohors I Barcinonum, Barcino Oriens from Catalonia (namely Marc Seriol), Legio VI Victrix Cohors II Cimbria from Scandinavia, Legio XI C.P.F. Hispaniensis from Spain (especially Iago Rodriguez Diaz), Legio XIII Gemina from Austria, Legio XIIII Gemina from the USA (in particular David Burns), Lorica Romana from France (especially Marilyn Paléri) and Insubria Gaesata from Italy.

# Introduction

The main aim of this book is to present a detailed overview of the history, organization and equipment of the Roman military forces during the period from 264–30 BC. This era, starting with the outbreak of the First Punic War and ending with the foundation of the Roman Empire, saw the ascendancy of the Roman Republic to be the major military power of the Mediterranean world. At the beginning of the period taken into account, the Romans did not have a fleet and were still completing their conquest of the Italian peninsula; by the end of it, they had no rivals and had organized their territorial possessions into a single centralized state. In this book we will pay particular attention to the organizational evolution of the Roman military and will detail the different pieces of equipment that were employed by the Romans during this period. At the same time, we will provide a general outline of all the external wars that were fought by the Roman Republic. For reasons of space and in order to follow Roman expansionism in as full detail as is possible, the many civil wars of the Roman Republic won't be covered in this book, but will be analysed in a separate volume. As a result, the present work will deal with the military campaigns fought by the Romans against the following external enemies: the Carthaginians, Celts, Illyrians, Macedonians, Spartans, Seleucids, Greeks, Galatians, Iberians, Germani, Numidians, Pontians and Parthians.

# Chapter 1

# The Roman Army of the Republic

During the decade from 335–325 BC, the Romans completely reformed their military forces by abandoning their old hoplite tactics and the general structure introduced by King Servius Tullius. The tactical formations based on the deployment of the phalanx on the open field had proved to be of very little use on the broken terrain of southern Italy, where they revealed all their deficiencies in terms of mobility. In order to fight and move more rapidly, the Roman legion had to be divided into smaller and more flexible sub-units, which could act as independent corps and operate not only in close formation but also as light infantry. To achieve this ambitious objective, the Romans decided to copy the best features of the military organization of the Samnites and to introduce these in their own armed forces. The Samnite armies had always been structured on small units of sixty warriors, called *manipuli* by the Romans: these extremely flexible corps were small enough to be assembled into larger formations but were also large enough to be employed in an autonomous way. Each *manipulus* could perform a specific task on the battlefield or garrison a particular location. In addition, all *manipuli* could be easily rotated during a battle in order to always have fresh troops on the front line. All these things were impossible or very difficult to do with a legion made up of *centuriae* (sub-units of 100 soldiers), since they were too large to perform specific duties and were not trained to operate as independent corps. Consequently, the great reform of the Roman Army that took place between the First and Second Samnite Wars is commonly known as the Manipular Reform, as it saw the rapid passage from a legion made up of *centuriae* to one composed of *manipuli*. This transition was not easy to complete, mostly because it took place together with a deep reform of Roman tactics and the adoption of new weapons by the whole Roman military machine. The Romans had understood that their subdivision of the infantry into five different 'classes' was completely outdated: the Samnites, for example, equipped all their warriors in a standard way as a sort of medium infantry which had javelins as their main weapon. The Roman heavy infantry of the hoplites were too slow to oppose the Samnite warriors on the open field and could use their traditional close formations only against the Etruscans or the Greeks, who still fought in the 'old' manner. The Roman light infantry of the lowest classes, meanwhile, were poorly equipped and trained compared to the Samnite skirmishers

Samnite warrior from the years of the Second Samnite War. (*Photo and copyright by Confraternita del Leone/Historia Viva*)

Apulian warrior. As is clear from the dolphin painted on his shield, he is an ally of the Greek city of Taras (whose traditional symbol was the dolphin). (*Photo and copyright by Hetairoi*)

Apulian warrior (left) and Lucanian warrior (right). The Lucanians were equipped very similarly to the Samnites, since they were an Oscan people like the latter. (*Photo and copyright by Hetairoi*)

(who were armed with javelins but had a helmet and armour). For these reasons, the Romans had to adopt new sets of equipment for their troops and replace their hoplite spears with javelins.

The original five classes of infantrymen were transformed into three new categories of foot troops: the *hastati*, the *principes* and the *triarii*. According to this new system, the categories of troops were not created by assembling soldiers from the same economic/social background, but by grouping together those of the same age and level of combat experience. The census was thus no longer the key factor in determining the tactical function and personal equipment of each troop type. The *hastati* were the youngest and least experienced soldiers of the Roman Army, having medium equipment in order to make good use of their agility. The *principes* were the strongest and best trained soldiers of the Army, with heavy equipment that included javelins. The *triarii* were the oldest and most experienced veterans, having heavy equipment that still comprised a hoplite spear. On most occasions, battles were fought only by the *hastati* and *principes*, there being no need to also employ the *triarii*, who acted as a sort of tactical reserve to be used only when absolutely necessary. If the *hastati* and *principes* were routed, for example, the *triarii* were deployed in phalanx formation in order to create a screen behind which the *hastati* and *principes* could retreat. In general, due to their equipment, the *triarii* could perform only static or defensive duties and were not suited to offensive operations. They were the last remnants of the Servian phalanx and a symbol of Roman military pride: being a *triarius* meant you were a veteran who had been strong enough to survive at least a dozen battles. Each of the new Roman legions was now to comprise a total of forty-five *manipuli*: fifteen of *hastati*, who formed the first line, fifteen of *principes*, who comprised the second line, and fifteen of *triarii*, who made up the third line. As a result, a manipular legion deployed a total of 2,700 medium/heavy infantrymen: 900 each of *hastati*, *principes* and *triarii*.

In addition to the *hastati*, *principes* and *triarii*, there were another three categories of combatants that were included in the early manipular legion: the *leves*, the *accensi* and the *rorarii*. These all had light personal equipment and thus could not be deployed in close formation. The *leves* were the light equivalent of the *hastati* in terms of age and combat experience, and supported the latter in the first line. Twenty *leves* were attached to each *manipulus* of *hastati* and acted as scouts or skirmishers. The *accensi* and the *rorarii*, instead, were the light equivalent of the *principes* and *triarii* in terms of age and battle experience. Each *manipulus* of *triarii* was reinforced by one *manipulus* of *accensi* and one of *rorarii*. The *leves* were the vanguard of the legion, while the *accensi* and the *rorarii* supported the *triarii* in the rear of the formation. Each legion comprised 300 *leves* (twenty for each *manipulus* of *hastati*), 900 *accensi* and 900 *rorarii*.

Macedonian phalangite from the years of the Second Macedonian War. (*Photo and copyright by Hetairoi*)

'Imitation legionary' (*thorakitai*) from one of the Hellenistic armies that fought against Rome during the Republican Period. (*Photo and copyright by Hetairoi*)

The transition from the Servian legion to the new manipular one happened as follows: the first three classes of infantrymen were transformed into the *hastati*, *principes* and *triarii*, the fourth class became the *accensi* and the fifth class the *rorarii*. The *leves* were a brand new category of troops who did not have their own separate *manipuli*. While the *accensi* and the *rorarii* maintained the personal equipment that was characteristic of the classes from which they came, the *leves* received the lightest personal equipment of the whole Roman Army. Consequently, it is clear that some distinctions related to the economic capabilities of each soldier continued to exist in the Roman Army: the rich citizens of the middle classes continued to serve in their own units, albeit now being organized according to their age and combat experience, while the poorer citizens still had their separate corps of light infantry (*leves*, *accensi* and *rorarii*). To sum up, a manipular Roman legion comprised 4,800 infantrymen organized into the following units: fifteen *manipuli* of eighty men each in the first line, fifteen *manipuli* of sixty men each in the second line and forty-five *manipuli* of sixty men each in the third line. As this makes clear, the rear of the legion comprised the largest number of soldiers, who were all employed only in case of need, since the *accensi* and the *rorarii* also made up a sort of reserve like the heavily equipped *triarii*. At the back of the legion, the forty-five reserve *manipuli* were deployed in three lines, or *ordines*: first came the fifteen units of *triarii*, then the fifteen units of *accensi* and finally the fifteen units of *rorarii*.

The manipular reform also affected the organization of the Roman cavalry, which now comprised 300 horsemen for each legion, assembled into ten *turmae* with thirty soldiers in each. The previous organization based on *centuriae* was also abandoned for the cavalry, although they continued to be made up of aristocrats and maintained their traditional panoply.

After the end of the last war fought against the Latins, around 335 BC, the Roman Army was greatly enlarged, with the two Servian legions being transformed into four manipular legions. Each of the two consuls was to command a consular army of two legions, in order to avoid a single man being able to control all the military power of Rome. Since each legion deployed 4,800 infantry and 300 cavalry, a consular army deployed 9,600 infantry and 600 cavalry. The whole Roman Army thus had 19,200 infantry and 1,200 cavalry. Their numbers were supplemented by large contingents sent by the allies, who started to be organized in a much more stable and standardized way after the dissolution of the Latin League. Around 335 BC, all the allies of Rome were forced to adopt the manipular system and had to organize their own forces in the Roman way. The legions provided by the allies were commonly known as *alae sociorum*, being deployed on the flanks of the Roman formations during battle. Their internal structure was slightly different from that of the Roman legions, since they contained a higher number of cavalrymen. Differently from the other Italic peoples, the Romans did not have a great cavalry tradition and preferred to fight on foot. As a result, starting a trend that would continue until the mid-centuries of the Roman Empire, Roman commanders preferred to employ cavalry contingents almost entirely formed by allied soldiers. Each *ala sociorum*, or allied legion, had 5,700 soldiers: 4,800 infantry and 900 cavalry. The infantrymen were organized exactly like those of a Roman legion, while the cavalry was structured on thirty *turmae* with thirty soldiers in each.

By the time of the Second Samnite War, the allies of Rome had been organized into four *alae sociorum*, two of which were included in each consular army. The *socii* of Rome therefore provided an impressive force of 22,800 soldiers (19,200 infantry and 3,600 cavalry), which with the 19,200 Roman infantry and 1,200 Roman cavalry gave a grand total of 43,300 combatants (4,800 of whom were mounted). On the battlefield, the soldiers of a consular army (9,600 Roman infantry, 600 Roman cavalry, 9,600 allied infantry and 1,800 allied cavalry) were deployed as follows: the infantry of the two Roman legions was in the centre, with one *ala sociorum* on each flank; the Roman cavalry made up the first line of each wing, with ten *turmae* on each side, while the allied cavalry made up the remaining three lines of each wing (each line comprising another ten *turmae*). After their first encounters with the Hellenistic phalanx of Pyrrhus, King of Epirus, the Romans realized that their manipular legion was too light to face a massive formation of well-trained heavy infantrymen on the open field. The manipular legion had been designed to fight against a highly mobile and lightly armed enemy like the Samnites, but in the near future the new enemies of the Romans would be the Hellenistic armies of the east that all deployed phalangists (pikemen) among their many military contingents. As a result, in order to update their manipular legion, the Romans had to carry out a new military reform. The first step of this change was to increase the number of soldiers in each *manipulus* from sixty to 120 so that the basic Roman unit would be large enough to face its equivalent in the Hellenistic phalanx (the *lochos*, or company, which had 128 heavy infantry). The internal structure of the light infantry contingents was completely changed, with the three existing categories (*leves*, *accensi* and *rorarii*) all abolished in order to create a single and unified light infantry corps: the *velites*. Consequently, the revised manipular legion started to be deployed on three lines (*acies*) as follows: the first line comprised ten *manipuli* of *hastati*, each supported by forty *velites*, for a total of 1,200 *hastati* and 400 *velites*; the second line had ten *manipuli* of *principes*, each supported by forty *velites*, for a total of 1,200 *principes* and 400 *velites*; the third line was composed of ten *manipuli* of *triarii*, each supported by forty *velites*. The *manipuli* of *triarii* remained of the old type, with just sixty soldiers in each, and were

Roman *velite* of the manipular legion. (*Photo and copyright by Aera Legio I Consularis*)

Roman *princeps* of the manipular legion. (*Photo and copyright by Aera Legio I Consularis*)

not expanded to 120 men, so the third line of a legion comprised only 600 *triarii* and 400 *velites*. In total, the infantry of a new manipular legion consisted of 4,200 men: 1,200 *velites*, 1,200 *hastati*, 1,200 *principes* and 600 *triarii*. As is clear from the above, the proportions of heavy infantry and light infantry had greatly changed: in the previous version of the manipular legion there were 2,700 heavy infantry and 2,100 light infantry; in the new one there were 3,000 heavy infantry and 1,200 light infantry. Light troops were fundamental for a campaign fought against the Oscan peoples on the broken terrain of Samnium, but were of little use against a Macedonian phalanx from Epirus.

In case of a national emergency, as happened during the Second Punic War with Hannibal's invasion of Italy, the infantry of a legion could be expanded to 5,100 men. This was done by adding 300 soldiers to the first line of *hastati*, 300 to the second line of *principes* and 300 to the *velites* (100 for each of the three *acies*). Tactically, the *velites* were of great use mostly before and after a battle. Before the clash they were tasked with explorative and skirmishing duties, while afterwards they could help the *triarii* in covering a retreat (in case of defeat) or attack a retreating enemy (in case of victory). During the battle itself, the light infantry initiated the clash by throwing their javelins to provoke the enemy. On some occasions, however, they could help their own cavalry against the mounted troops of the enemy or attack the flanks of the Hellenistic war elephants. The Roman cavalry was not affected by the military reform described above: it continued to be organized on ten *turmae*, with thirty men in each, for each legion. The new manipular legion therefore had exactly 4,500 soldiers: 4,200 infantry and 300 cavalry. The *alae sociorum*, the legions of the allies, adopted the new organizational system introduced for the Roman Army but continued to have 900 horsemen each instead of the standard 300. During the military emergency caused by the Epirote invasion of Italy, Rome mobilized all its available resources and was able to deploy in the field two consular armies with six legions each: instead of the usual armies with two Roman and two allied legions, the Romans deployed consular armies with four Roman and two allied legions each.

# Chapter 2

# The First Punic War

With the defeat of Pyrrhus and the Greek colony of Tarentum, Rome acquired control over all the continental territory of southern Italy. The Greek cities of the region were forced to recognize the Romans as their formal protectors and the local Oscan peoples (the Lucanians and the Bruttii) became *socii* of the Roman Republic. Since Etruria had been conquered earlier and the Picentes were already allies of Rome, most of the Italian peninsula was under Roman control. Only two areas were still independent: northern Italy (inhabited by several Celtic tribes) and the islands of Sicily, Sardinia and Corsica. The first target of the Romans, after conquering Tarentum in 272 BC, was Sicily, the most fertile region of Italy which produced large amounts of top-quality grain. In addition, thanks to its key location in the centre of the Mediterranean, it could be employed as a perfect base for further expansionist campaigns. From a political point of view, Sicily was extremely fragmented: the western part of the island was in the hands of the Carthaginians, who also controlled Sardinia and Corsica; the central and eastern parts, meanwhile, were ruled by Syracuse, which had gradually imposed its dominance over all the other Greek cities of Sicily. The Carthaginians (called *Punici* by the Romans) and the Syracusans were constantly at war against each other. Since 289 BC, this difficult political situation had been further complicated by the appearance of a new military player: the Mamertini. These were Italic mercenaries, mostly Oscans, who had been contracted by Syracuse in order to fight against the Carthaginians. At that time Syracuse's army was mostly composed of mercenaries from every corner of the Mediterranean; the Mamertini, whose name meant 'sons of Mars', were the most effective and violent of these. When in 289 BC the Syracusan tyrant who had contracted them died, the Mamertini became a problem for the new government of the Greek city, which disbanded the large mercenary army that had been employed against the Carthaginians and paid off the Mamertini for their services. While marching back to their homeland, however, the Oscan mercenaries decided to remain in Sicily in order to create their own independent settlement on the island. They assaulted and conquered Messana with a surprise attack, thus becoming the rulers of the strait that separated mainland Italy from Sicily. The Mamertini soon transformed themselves into pirates and started to attack all the merchant ships passing through the Strait of Messana. This situation was unacceptable for the Syracusans, who tried without success to destroy the Mamertini on several occasions. When Pyrrhus came to Sicily during his Italian campaigns, the ex-mercenaries formed an alliance with the Carthaginians. In the following months they were defeated in battle on several occasions by the Epirotes, but were able to retain control of Messana until Pyrrhus was forced by events to leave Sicily. In the years following the withdrawal of Pyrrhus, the Mamertini continued to be supported by the Carthaginians and became even stronger. Soon after the departure of the Epirotes, the city of Rhegion also came under control of the former mercenaries. During the war against Pyrrhus, the Romans had garrisoned Rhegion with a legion of allies formed by Campanians. The city was located across from Messana on mainland Italy and thus controlled the other side of the strait. After the Epirotes abandoned Sicily, the Campanian legionaries revolted against Rome and killed their officers. They proclaimed the independence of Rhegion and formed an alliance with their Oscan 'brothers' in Messana. As a result of these events, the Mamertini formed a piratical kingdom that was centred around the Strait of Messana. In 270 BC, concerned by these events, the Romans decided to intervene and sent an army against Rhegion, which was besieged and reconquered, with the help of Syracuse. At this point the Romans could have sent their troops across to Sicily to help the Syracusans against the Mamertini of Messana, but since the latter city was located outside mainland Italy, such a Roman intervention would have represented a violation of the treaty existing between the Romans and the Carthaginians (which included Sicily in Carthage's sphere of influence).

During the following years, the Syracusans tried to defeat the Mamertini alone, obtaining a decisive victory on the open field against them in 265 BC. At this point, being on the verge of destruction, the Oscan pirates formally requested Carthaginian military help. The Carthaginians sent a fleet and installed a small garrison in Messana. The Syracusans, being in no position to fight alone against Carthage in a new war, suspended their military operations against the Mamertini. Rome then decided to intervene in Sicily in order to avoid the Carthaginians gaining complete dominance over the Strait of Messana by 'using' the Mamertini. In 264 BC, using as a *casus belli* a request for help sent by some Mamertini who were hostile to the Carthaginians, Rome sent an army against Messana and thus initiated the First Punic War against Carthage. The Romans easily crushed the Mamertini and occupied Messana before the Carthaginians could react. Rome now controlled both sides of the strait and had an important base from which to conquer the rest of Sicily. Fearing that most of their territory could soon be occupied by the Romans, the Syracusans decided to ally themselves with their former Carthaginian enemies. Before the Carthaginians and Syracusans could join forces, the Romans defeated a Syracusan army and then moved

Roman *princeps*; note the leather protection for the shoulders attached on the chainmail. (*Photo and copyright by Aera Legio I Consularis*)

against a Carthaginian one that was marching against Messana. After also defeating the Carthaginians, the Romans secured their control over Messana and then started besieging Syracuse. The Syracusans, being on the verge of defeat, concluded a truce with the Romans in order to preserve their independence and thereby changed sides in the war. Subsequently, employing the resources of their new allies, the Romans moved to conquer the central part of Sicily. The Carthaginians assembled most of their forces in the important city of Agrigento, which was besieged for seven months by the Romans before being taken in 261 BC.

By this point of the First Punic War, the Romans had obtained a series of clear victories on land, but the Carthaginians were still the masters of the Mediterranean Sea. Rome had never previously had a proper military fleet, being able to deploy only a very limited number of small warships. The landing in Sicily had only been possible thanks to the decisive naval support received from the allied Greek cities of southern Italy, which gave the Roman forces in Sicily all the logistic support they needed. If the Romans wanted to defeat the Carthaginians at sea, however, they would need to have a fleet of their own. Achieving such a feat was not a simple undertaking, for several reasons. First of all, building an entire fleet from scratch and in a short time had enormous costs; secondly, the Romans had no experience of naval combat and knew practically nothing of Carthaginian tactics; finally, the Romans did not have any naval bases and thus depended on their Greek allies for the construction and repair of warships. Despite all these problems, the Roman Republic was able in just a few months to build a fleet of 120 warships in the Greek arsenals of southern Italy and to train 30,000 Italic peasants as sailors. The first naval battle between Romans and Carthaginians took place off the Aeolian Islands in 260 BC and ended in defeat for Rome. After this initial failure, however, the Romans rapidly learned from their experience and were able to defeat a Carthaginian fleet at Milazzo. The Roman success was determined by the use of the corvus, a new boarding device that was unknown to the Carthaginians and which consisted of a mobile wooden bridge with a heavy spike on the underside. By using the corvus, the Romans could block and board a Carthaginian warship, thereby in effect transforming a naval clash into a land battle during which the legionaries could employ their superior weapons and tactics as if they were fighting on *terra firma*. After obtaining their first naval victory, the Romans also sent troops to Sardinia and Corsica to expand the conflict to the whole central part of the Mediterranean.

In 257 BC, with a new and larger fleet, the Romans tried to end the war by invading North Africa with an army of 97,000 soldiers. The Carthaginians attempted to prevent the invasion by assembling a fleet of 250 warships with 150,000 men. In the ensuing Battle of Cape Ecnomus, the greatest naval clash of Antiquity, the Romans obtained

Roman *princeps*; note the brass plaque applied on the front of the chainmail. (*Photo and copyright by Aera Legio I Consularis*)

Roman *princeps* wearing pteruges made of red leather in addition to his chainmail. (*Photo and copyright by Aera Legio I Consularis*)

a clear victory, destroying most of the enemy vessels. After disembarking in Africa, the Roman army obtained some minor victories and menaced the city of Carthage. Hostilities were then temporarily suspended to allow peace negotiations, but these produced no results. When hostilities were resumed, the Carthaginians reorganized their land forces in Africa by putting them under the command of a mercenary Spartan general named Xanthippus. The new leader completely reorganized the Carthaginian Army along Hellenistic lines in a very short time and was able to route the Romans at the Battle of Tunis in 255 BC. The few surviving Roman soldiers were forced to abandon North Africa, but during the journey back to Sicily the entire Roman fleet was destroyed by a terrible storm. In 253 BC the Romans made another attempt to disembark their troops in Africa, but the campaign was also a failure and the fleet was destroyed by a storm while returning to Sicily.

The situation of the armies in Sicily, meanwhile, had not changed to any great extent, with the Romans controlling the eastern territories and the Carthaginians the western ones. In 249 BC, the Roman fleet, which had been rebuilt, was destroyed again by Carthage at the Battle of Trapani, after which the war saw no major battle on land or sea for six years as both Rome and Carthage had used up all their available resources. In 242 BC, the Romans were finally able to build a new fleet and during the following year obtained a clear victory over the enemy navy at the Battle of the Aegades Islands. This clash marked the end of the First Punic War, since Carthage was no longer in any condition to continue the fight. Rome obtained much from the subsequent peace treaty, with the Carthaginians forced to evacuate Sicily and to pay an immense war indemnity. During the following years, the Carthaginian state was bankrupted by the financial burden caused by the payment of the indemnity. This had very negative consequences for the Carthaginian empire in the Mediterranean, since there was not enough money to build new warships or to pay the thousands of mercenaries who made up the Carthaginian Army. The mercenaries soon revolted against their masters and ravaged most of present-day Tunisia before being defeated by the Carthaginians. This episode, known as the Revolt of the Mercenaries, had some important consequences for the islands of the Mediterranean. With the Carthaginians temporarily without a fleet and the city of Carthage menaced by the rebelling mercenaries, Rome could transform Sicily into its first province and also send military expeditions to the other islands. According to the peace treaty that concluded the First Punic War, Sicily was to remain a neutral zone between the Roman and Carthaginian possessions. However, after the Carthaginians abandoned the island, the Romans occupied most of it except for Syracuse, which was transformed into a Roman protectorate. With the outbreak of the Second Punic War, Syracuse would revolt against the Romans, but it was eventually conquered and annexed to the

Roman *princeps* with Montefortino helmet. (*Photo and copyright by Patrick Thierry*)

Roman province of Sicily. In Sardinia and Corsica, the situation was rather different. Here, the local Carthaginian garrisons, which had not been defeated by the Romans during the course of the first war, were entirely made up of mercenaries. When these were not paid by Carthage at the end of hostilities, they revolted like their comrades in North Africa and devastated most of the areas in which they were garrisoned. Taking advantage of this situation by presenting itself as the defender of the local Sardinian and Corsican peoples, Rome sent military expeditions to both islands and occupied them after defeating the rebellious mercenaries.

Starting from around 1,600 BC, the people of Sardinia had developed a very advanced culture known as the Nuragic civilization, derived from the word *nuraghe* (massive stone towers that were built in great numbers in every corner of Sardinia). The Sardinians lived in isolated settlements that had more or less the dimensions of a village. They were all shepherds and their economy was thus a very simple one. They were very good at working metal and had important commercial contacts with the other peoples of the Mediterranean. Around the ninth century BC, the first Phoenician colonists reached Sardinia and started to build outposts on the coast of the island. Like the Etruscans in Corsica, the Phoenicians wanted to use Sardinia as an important base for their naval activities. When the various Phoenician settlements of the island came under the control of Carthage, the foreign presence in Sardinia became much more significant. Over time, the Carthaginians discovered that Sardinia was full of potential for mining precious metals and thus tried to penetrate into the interior of the island; here, however, they met strong resistance from local warriors who had a very warlike nature and were equipped with high quality weapons. The broken terrain of Sardinia, with no roads and being covered by hills, was perfect to organize a strong resistance using guerrilla tactics. In 535 BC, the Carthaginians landed a large army on the island in a bid to subjugate its people, but after twenty-five years of skirmishing and ambushes they were only able to conquer the south-western half of Sardinia. In subsequent decades the Sardinians revolted on several occasions, angered by the high level of taxation imposed by the Carthaginians and their use of the local populace as virtual slaves in order to extract natural resources from the mines. By the outbreak of the First Punic War, the portion of Sardinia that was under Carthaginian control had developed a distinctive mixed civilization comprising both Punic and local elements. As we have seen, the Romans arrived in Sardinia after the island's Carthaginian garrison of mercenaries mutinied. However, the Sardinians opposed the Roman occupation just as they had resisted against the Carthaginians. In 215 BC, under the guidance of their warlord Ampsicora, the entire population rebelled and attacked the Roman occupiers. As Rome was at the time experiencing serious military difficulties against Hannibal in Italy, it could not send reinforcements to Sardinia. The Carthaginians, meanwhile, landed 15,000 soldiers on the island to support the rebellion. Eventually, however, Ampsicora was utterly defeated by the Romans in a decisive and bloody battle at Decimomannu. This clash marked the end of the Carthaginian presence in Sardinia. The local population continued for decades to wage a fierce guerrilla war against the Romans, retaining control of the island's interior, which started to be known as the *Barbagia* (Latin for 'land of the barbarians'). In an attempt to crush the resistance, the Romans enslaved thousands of Sardinians and transferred them to mainland Italy, but it was only in 111 BC that the island was finally pacified by the Republic.

# Chapter 3

# The Conquest of Gallia Cisalpina and the Illyrian Wars

Through its ultimate victory in the First Punic War, Rome had definitively transformed itself from a regional power into a Mediterranean one, with the only part of Italy that was still free from its rule being the vast northern area dominated by the Celtic tribes. In 249 BC, the Celts of Cisalpine Gaul ('Gaul south of the Alps'), coming under strong Roman pressure and hoping to take advantage of the ongoing conflict between Rome and Carthage, decided to ask for help against Rome from their 'cousins' of Transalpine Gaul ('Gaul north of the Alps'). The Celts from present-day France, being in search of new lands to solve their problems of overpopulation, gave a positive response to this request and sent a large army into northern Italy. According to ancient sources, this force comprised 50,000 warriors on foot and 25,000 horsemen. With the help of these reinforcements, the Italian Celts were able to resume hostilities against the Roman Republic. We have no precise details about these 75,000 warriors who subsequently moved south towards Italy: ancient writers call them *Gaesatae*, using a term that probably meant 'mercenaries' in the Celtic language. This seems to confirm that the *Gaesatae* were not migrating to Italy with their families and goods, but were probably warriors who had been recruited by Cisalpine emissaries. The population of Transalpine Gaul was at the time greatly increasing and there were too few resources to sustain such a large number of inhabitants. Minor warlords and young warriors were in search of new opportunities and new lands, their home territory having little more to offer, so the Cisalpine Gauls had no problems in raising a large army of 75,000 mercenaries from north of the Alps. These warriors looked more 'barbarian' to the Romans than those living in northern Italy, having experienced very little contact with the Mediterranean world and thus preserved their original Celtic identity.

The Republic was surprised by the arrival of such a large military force from Gaul and initially had serious problems in containing the Celts. The new hostilities between Romans and Gauls were prolonged, lasting until 225 BC. The *Gaesatae* proved to be excellent warriors, defeating armies of the Republic on several occasions. In 225 BC, however, a decisive clash between the Romans and Celts was fought at Telamon, where, like at Sentinum some 70 years before, the battle ended in complete disaster for the Gauls, who suffered enormous losses. The military potential of the *Gaesatae*

Celtic warlord from Gallia Cisalpina, wearing leather cuirass. (*Photo and copyright by Luca Brizzi of the Historical Reconstitution Association Insubria Gaesata*)

Celtic warrior from Gallia Cisalpina, wearing Montefortino helmet and padded cuirass. (*Photo and copyright by Luca Brizzi of the Historical Reconstitution Association Insubria Gaesata*)

Celtic warrior from Provence, armed with spear and long sword. (*Photo and copyright by Teuta Arverni*)

had been broken, but the same could not be said of the Cisalpine Gauls' spirit. In 223 BC, in an attempt to crush the resistance of their enemy, the Romans sent an army of 40,000 soldiers to invade northern Italy. The Republic's offensive proved successful from the outset, many Celtic tribesmen having decided to side with Rome (hoping to thereby acquire new lands). During the following year, another major pitched battle was fought between Romans and Gauls at Clastidium, the Cisalpine Celts again suffering defeat and their whole territory in northern Italy being occupied by Rome (including the important centre of Mediolanum). Cisalpine Gaul had now fallen and the Romans were the new masters of the Italian peninsula. The Celts, however, had surrendered only because they had no more resources to continue the fight, and at the first opportunity would revolt again against Rome to regain their freedom. It is important to note, however, that the smaller Celtic communities living in the Italian Alps continued to fight against the Romans (albeit with guerrilla methods). These Alpine groups, having settled in Italy for many years, had no intention of giving up their mountain passes. The Romans were still in the process of submitting them when a great foreign warlord arrived to lead the Celts in their revenge: Hannibal Barca, the great Carthaginian general. Hannibal proclaimed himself a friend of the Celts, many of whom soon flocked to his banners. Under the guidance of such a capable and intelligent military leader, the Celts fought magnificently on several occasions, providing a vital contribution to Hannibal's great victories on Italian soil. By 215 BC, it seemed that the Romans were no longer in any condition to reconquer northern Italy from the Gauls, Rome being menaced by the Carthaginians and all the peoples of Italy who were now fighting on Hannibal's side.

As we will see, however, this state of affairs changed quite rapidly and most of the Carthaginian forces were obliged to leave Italy in order to defend their homeland in Africa. In 202 BC, Hannibal was decisively defeated by the Romans at the Battle of Zama, but this event did not lead to the surrender of the Italian Celts. The people of Cisalpine Gaul had no intention of giving up their new-found freedom, which had been obtained through many sacrifices. Consequently, also thanks to the presence of Carthaginian troops that were still stationed on their territory, they decided to continue hostilities against Rome. Nevertheless, at the Battle of Cremona in 200 BC, the Celts and their Carthaginian and Ligurian allies were defeated by the Romans in a clash that proved to be decisive for the destiny of Cisalpine Gaul. Although the campaign continued until 194 BC, the Celts were no longer in a position to contest Roman dominance over their lands in northern Italy. After the end of the Second Punic War, the Celts of southern France started to experience more direct contact with Rome. The Greek colony of Massalia (present-day Marseille), Rome's most loyal ally in southern France, started to experience serious difficulty in containing the incursions of neighbouring Celtic tribes.

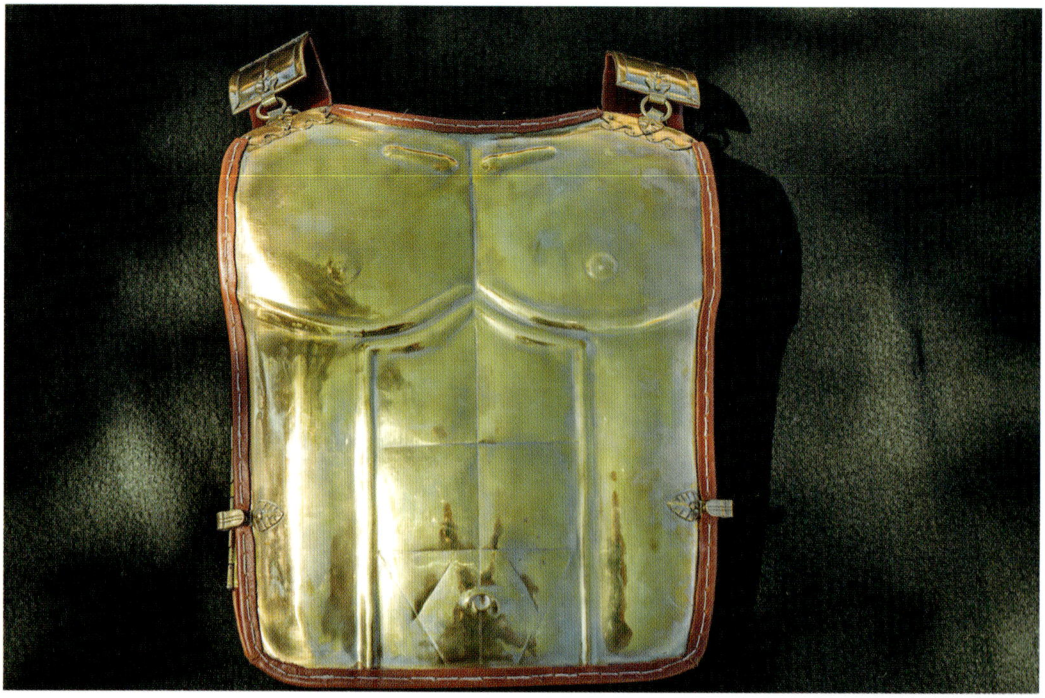

Detail of the muscle cuirass in Oscan style employed by the Roman *hastati*. (*Photo by Diego Casillas and copyright by Divulgación Histórica TANIT*)

The Gauls, however, were not the only menace for Massalia: the Ligurians, who lived on Gaul's Mediterranean coast, were also a serious threat to the security of the Greek city. Ligurian pirates frequently assaulted the merchant ships arriving at or departing from Massalia, making the vital trade routes of the city extremely dangerous. In 181 BC, at the request of Massalia, Rome sent military forces to destroy the Ligurian pirates, the Republic having strong interests in that area of the Mediterranean (especially after the conquest of Sardinia and Corsica). In 154 BC, the Romans mounted another expedition against the Ligurian tribes of southern France, in collaboration with their Massalian allies. This time the defeat of the pirates was decisive, allowing the Greek colony to resume control over commercial routes in the area. During the following decades, however, this region of southern Gaul continued to experience internal tensions, with the Celts starting to increase their pressure on Massalia by launching more frequent and more destructive raids. By 125 BC, a confederation of various tribes, collectively known as the Salyens, threatened the city of Massalia. Rome once again decided to intervene to save its Greek allies, but already had in mind to expel the Celts from most of southern Gaul. After two years of harsh campaigning, Roman forces destroyed the Salyens and captured their capital. However, the newly conquered territories were not given to Massalia but

Celtic warrior from Provence, equipped with spear and shield. (*Photo and copyright by Teuta Arverni*)

were annexed by the Republic (the Romans even founded a colony on the former homeland of the Salyens, which would later be known as Aix-en-Provence). In 122 BC, the remaining forces of the Salyens revolted against Rome and were joined by powerful Celtic tribes from other areas of Gaul (the Arverni and the Allobroges).

Celtic warrior from the Balkans, standing in front of a fortified village. (*Photo and copyright by Ancient Thrace*)

During 122 and 121 BC, the Romans had to use large military resources to subdue the Celts of southern France, who surrendered only after having been defeated in two major pitched battles which caused them enormous losses. After these victories, the Romans annexed all the Celtic lands located between Iberia and northern Italy: only Massalia remained formally independent, albeit being practically surrounded by Roman territories. The territories of Rome in southern Gaul soon became known as Provence, since they were organized as one of the Republic's provinces.

In addition to the Celts, the Romans had another deadly enemy just outside the borders of the Italian peninsula: the Illyrians in the western Balkans. An extremely warlike people, they lived on the harsh terrain of the Balkan mountains and the vast coastline of modern Croatia. The Illyrians were originally organized as independent tribes, but various leagues of tribes started to emerge in the western Balkans and the first Illyrian kingdoms then appeared. The early disputes between the Roman Republic and the Illyrians were caused by the latter's favourite activity: piracy. The Adriatic Sea separating the Italian peninsula from the Balkans was infested by Illyrian pirates, who had their bases on the many small islands of present-day Croatia. Using small but agile vessels, the Illyrians attacked transport ships crossing the Adriatic Sea and stole any profitable goods they came across. The Adriatic was criss-crossed by the commercial routes that connected Roman territory with Greece, and thus was of fundamental importance for the expanding Roman economy. Attacks by the Illyrian pirates caused great damage to Roman merchants, gradually becoming a serious problem for the Republic. Before the outbreak of the First Punic War, Rome did not have a fleet and thus was unable to fight against the Illyrians at sea. After the end of that conflict, however, the Romans could finally employ their recently built warships against the pirates in the Adriatic. By 240 BC, the most important kingdom of the Illyrians was that of the Ardiaei, which had become a formidable naval power under the strong leadership of King Agron. The Ardiaei attacked the Hellenistic Kingdom of Epirus from the north, occupied several Greek islands (including Corcyra and Pharos) and established new naval bases in the southern Adriatic. Using the *lembus*, a small and fast warship with a single bank of oars that could carry fifty warriors in addition to the rowers, the Illyrians launched raids against the eastern coastline of the Italian peninsula and the Greek Ionian Islands. In 232 BC, the Ardiaei invaded Epirus with an army of 5,000 warriors, taking advantage of the political chaos that had emerged in the kingdom due to a dynastic crisis. Against all odds, the invaders won a great victory against an army that had been sent against them by the Aetolian League. This event shocked the Greeks, who had never considered the Ardiaei as a major military power. In 231 BC, a large Illyrian fleet attacked Elis and Messenia in the Peloponnese, causing devastation and spreading panic in Greece. Agron had died

Roman *hastati*; the one on the left has muscle cuirass, while that on the right wears a simple rectangular plate of bronze on the chest. (*Photo and copyright by Aera Legio I Consularis*)

a few months before, with overall command assumed by his widow, Queen Teuta, who swiftly demonstrated she was a capable leader. Teuta later conquered Phoenice, the most prosperous coastal city of Epirus and the centre of the growing commerce with Italy. Fearing that the Ardiaei could now assume complete control over the Adriatic, the Roman Republic decided to intervene.

The First Illyrian War began in 229 BC with a Roman surprise invasion of Illyrian territory. The Ardiaei were at the time fighting against the Greeks for possession of

Roman *hastatus*; note the leather cover of the shield. (*Photo and copyright by Aera Legio I Consularis*)

the islands along the coastline of the Gulf of Corinth, and thus were not prepared for an invasion of their lands. The Roman consul Gnaeus Fulvius Centumalus was sent with a fleet of 200 ships to occupy the island of Corcyra, while consul Lucius Postumius brought an army of 22,000 soldiers to Apollonia with orders to invade the Illyrian homeland. After joining their forces, the two consuls advanced on the city of Epidamnos and captured it after expelling its Illyrian garrison. Having consolidated their control over the Epirote coastline, the Romans moved into the enemy hinterland. At this point some of the Illyrian tribes opposing the power of the Ardiaei decided to join the invaders, but the legionaries still encountered stiff opposition during their advance. While their land forces marched across the Illyrian interior, the Roman fleet attacked the coastal settlements and bases of the Illyrians, destroying many of them. Teuta, under great pressure, retreated to her capital of Rhizon in the Gulf of Kotor. At this point the Romans decided to stop their invasion, their objectives having been reached: they had no intention of annexing Illyria to their dominions, just wishing to destroy the naval bases of the pirates who infested the Adriatic. A peace treaty was concluded between Rome and the Ardiaei in 228 BC, according to which Teuta was to pay an indemnity to the Republic and to abandon most of her naval bases in Illyria. With their victory in the First Illyrian War, the Romans had greatly limited the expansionist ambitions of the Ardiaei, who – according to the peace treaty that ended the conflict – could not sail south of Lissus (present-day Alessio in northern Albania) with more than two unarmed ships. The terms of the treaty were welcomed in Greece, with the Illyrian menace being largely cancelled. However, the Illyrians soon started plotting their revenge, never accepting that the Romans had obliged them to give up all their recent conquests. Apollonia, Epidamnos and Corcyra were now in Roman hands, several Illyrian tribes had become clients of the Republic and there were fears that the Romans could soon occupy more Illyrian lands. As a result, the decade after 229 BC saw a revival of the Ardiei's power under Demetrius, the successor of Teuta.

Demetrius formed a strong military alliance with the Kingdom of Macedonia, and in 222 BC participated with 1,600 of his best warriors in the Battle of Sellasia that was fought between the Macedonians and Spartans. Under their new king, the Ardiaei gradually resumed their piratical activities, once again attacking Roman vessels. In 220 BC, an Illyrian fleet with ninety armed ships sailed south of Lissus and assaulted Pylos in the Peloponnese, the expedition later plundering the Cyclades and several Greek ports. Later that year, the Ardiaei attacked Roman client communities in southern Illyria, causing the outbreak of the Second Illyrian War. Unlike Teuta, however, Demetrius was well prepared for a Roman invasion. This time the Roman forces were led by the consul Aemilius Paulus, an experienced commander who decided to attack the important city of Dimallum. This was siezed by the legionaries

Roman *hastatus* of the manipular legion. (*Photo and copyright by Aera Legio I Consularis*)

in just seven days, despite being well garrisoned. Demetrius, with his best troops, was on the island of Pharos, which was soon attacked from two sides by the Romans and conquered in 218 BC after some fierce fighting. Demetrius managed to escape and fled to Macedonia, but his military forces had been completely destroyed. The Romans restored the status quo in the Adriatic and secured all the gains that they had obtained with the First Illyrian War. Demetrius was replaced as king of the Ardiaei by a younger monarch who was pro-Roman and agreed to pay the arrears of the indemnity that had been imposed on his people by the peace treaty of 228 BC.

Due to the outbreak of the Second Punic War, relations between the Romans and Illyrians remained quite positive until 170 BC, with no piratical attacks taking place in the Adriatic. In 168 BC, however, the Illyrian king Gentius formed a military alliance with Perseus V of Macedonia: he intended to resume piratical raids but needed money to equip his new warships. The Macedonians, who were fighting against Rome for dominance over Greece, had plenty of money but needed allies. Consequently, a powerful anti-Roman alliance was formed between Gentius and Perseus. The Illyrian monarch had worked hard in recent years to centralize the institutions of his state (for example by reforming the taxation system) and rebuild a large fleet. He could count on an army of some 15,000 warriors and a fleet with 270 *lembi*. In early 168 BC, Gentius attacked the Illyrian allies of Rome with his land forces and sent a small fleet to ravage the coastal settlements of Epidamnos and Apollonia. Rome reacted rapidly to these events, two legions crossing the Adriatic from Italy to Apollonia and joining forces with the Roman contingents that were already stationed in Epirus. A naval battle between Gentius' fleet and the Roman warships took place during the early phase of the conflict and ended with a clear Roman victory. The Illyrians were later also defeated on land, which allowed the Romans to advance to the very heart of Gentius' kingdom. The Illyrians concentrated their remaining forces in their capital of Shkodra, which was well fortified, but instead of resisting the Roman besiegers they swiftly surrendered. Gentius was not captured, but the Ardiaei had once again been defeated. All the treasures of the Illyrians, the result of many years of incursions in the Adriatic, were siezed by the Romans, together with a total of 220 enemy vessels. Gentius died shortly after the end of hostilities, thereby ending any hope of further Illyrian resistance. The small tribal kingdoms of Illyria were transformed into client states of the Republic and forced to pay a yearly tribute to Rome. Illyria had finally been conquered.

# Chapter 4

# The Second and Third Punic War

Following the end of the First Punic War, Carthage suffered a series of internal problems. First of all, there was a massive revolt by the mercenaries who had taken part in the conflict against Rome but had not been paid by the Carthaginian authorities. The professional soldiers mutinied against their former employers in what was known as the Mercenary War, or Truceless War, which was so serious for the state that it almost caused the destruction of Carthage. The massive military revolt was eventually crushed by Hamilcar Barca in 237 BC, but the Roman Republic took advantage of the Carthaginian difficulties at this time to annex both Sardinia and Corsica. Following these events, Hamilcar became the most important political and military leader in Carthage, being the first to understand that his city needed to find new economic and military resources if it wanted to fight a new war against Rome. These resources could be found only in Iberia (modern Spain), where Carthage already had several important bases. Iberia was full of natural resources that just needed to be exploited and was also a land of fierce warriors, who could be recruited by the Carthaginians as mercenaries or allies. In around ten years of harsh campaigning against the Iberian tribes, Hamilcar was able to conquer most of south-eastern Iberia for Carthage. Thanks to his personal charisma and diplomatic intelligence, he then transformed the most powerful local tribes into Carthaginian allies and submitted with harsh methods the communities that resisted his rule. In 226 BC, as a result of Hamilcar's expansion in Iberia, Rome and Carthage signed the Ebro Treaty, according to which the Ebro River was to mark the border between Carthaginian Spain and independent Iberia. In 220 BC, however, Rome formed a military alliance with the important Iberian city of Saguntum that was situated south of the Ebro River. Meanwhile, Hamilcar had died while crossing a river and command of the Carthaginian armies in Iberia had been assumed by his son, Hannibal. Extremely ambitious and audacious, Hannibal launched an attack on Saguntum in 219 BC. The city was captured and sacked after a lengthy siege, the Carthaginians clearly being in search of a *casus belli* with which to resume hostilities with the Roman Republic. Rome indeed declared war on Carthage in 218 BC, initiating the Second Punic War.

Initially military operations in the conflict were favourable to the Romans, who repulsed a Carthaginian attack against western Sicily and captured the strategically

Celtiberian warlord equipped with padded armour. (*Photo and copyright by Terra Carpetana*)

Roman *hastatus* throwing one of his javelins; note the practice of wearing a single greave on the leg not protected by the shield. (*Photo and copyright by Aera Legio I Consularis*)

important island of Malta. Rome was assembling a large army to be sent to Iberia to punish Hannibal for his actions, but before the expedition could leave Italy there was a major revolt of the Celts of Gallia Cisalpina, a region of northern Italy that had not yet been fully pacified by the Romans. Realizing that the Italian peninsula was vulnerable and that it could be invaded from the north, Hannibal decided to try something that had never been attempted before: marching a large army from southern Spain to northern Italy, crossing both the Pyrenees and the Alps. As Roman war fleets controlled the Mediterranean , making a seaborne Carthaginian invasion of Italy impossible, Rome was sure that its territory could never be attacked by the Carthaginians. Against all odds, however, and to Rome's astonishment, Hannibal crossed the Pyrenees at the head of some 40,000 infantry, 12,000 cavalry and 38 war elephants, and entered southern Gaul, where he fought a major battle against local Celt tribesmen to cross the River Rhone. The Carthaginians reached the Alps by late autumn and crossed them after surmounting enormous logistical difficulties, as well as defeating the resistance of various Celtic communities. When Hannibal descended from the Alps into northern Italy, he commanded an army that had shrunk to only about 26,000 warriors (20,000 infantry and 6,000 horsemen) and just a few surviving elephants. After fighting several minor clashes against the Celts of Cisalpine Gaul, the Carthaginian warlord formed a strong anti-Roman alliance with them and could start moving south. He first encountered a Roman army at the Battle of the Ticinus, routing it thanks to his brilliant battlefield tactics. This was an important victory, since it convinced all the Celts in Italy to join the invading Carthaginians. The Romans tried to stop Hannibal again by combining their forces in northern Italy with another army that had been sent to Sicily in view of a planned Roman invasion of North Africa. The unified Roman army, however, was crushed by Hannibal at the Battle of the Trebia, where of the 42,000 Roman soldiers who took part in the clash, only 10,000 survived. Following his second victory in Italy, Hannibal wintered in the north of the peninsula and recruited more Celtic tribesmen, increasing the number of warriors under his command to 60,000.

Following the Battle of the Trebia, the Romans recruited more legions and formed two new armies: one was to guard the land route connecting northern and central Italy along the western coastline of the peninsula, and the other that along the eastern coast. Hannibal, however, surprised his opponents by crossing the Apennines mountain range between the two coastal routes, and thus entered central Italy unopposed in the early spring of 217 BC. The Carthaginians cut off one of the two Roman armies (the largest one) from their capital and destroyed it at the Battle of the Trasimene, where the Romans were ambushed and suffered enormous casualties (around 15,000 killed and 10,000 captured). Following this victory, Hannibal continued his march south without meeting opposition and entered Apulia, in the hope of convincing most of the local Italic and Greek communities to rebel against Rome and join his cause. After the Battle of the Trasimene, the shell-shocked Romans elected a dictator – Quintus Fabius Maximus – and adopted a new strategy that included avoiding pitched battles in order to harass the enemy with guerrilla tactics. In 216 BC, however, two new consuls with much more aggressive military plans were elected: Gaius Terentius Varro and Lucius Aemilius Paulus. The pair were authorized by the Senate to raise a large army of 86,000 men and marched against Hannibal in Apulia. Here, however, they were annihilated at the Battle of Cannae. During the battle, the Roman legions forced their way through the Carthaginians' deliberately weak centre but were then surrounded by the enemy infantry deployed on their flanks. When Hannibal's cavalry attacked the legionaries from the rear after having routed the Roman mounted contingent, a massacre ensued. After it was over, around 67,000 Romans had been killed or captured in what was the greatest disaster in the military history of Rome.

Celtiberian warrior armed with thrusting spear and throwing javelin. (*Photo and copyright by Terra Carpetana*)

Celtiberian swordsman bearing large oval shield. (*Photo and copyright by Terra Carpetana*)

After the Battle of Cannae, the peoples of southern Italy deserted Rome and joined the foreign invaders, in the hope that the Carhaginians could free them from Roman dominance. Capua and Tarentum, two of the richest and largest cities of the region, allied themselves with Hannibal; Capua, in particular, became the main base of the Carthaginians in Italy. At this point of the war, however, Hannibal found himself in a difficult situation: he had defeated the Romans on several occasions and had occupied a good portion of Italy, but was in no conditions to attack the well-fortified city of Rome. The Carthaginian leader asked for reinforcements from his homeland on several occasions, but received only a few thousand soldiers from the government of Carthage. Being more interested in military operations that were taking place on other fronts, most notably in Spain, Carthage had no intention of wasting more resources in Italy. Meanwhile, the Roman Republic took drastic steps to raise new legions, which included enrolling the poorest citizens and even slaves. For eleven years after the Battle of Cannae, military operations surged around southern Italy, where the Carthaginians occupied several cities that were soon retaken by the Romans. It was a long period of sieges and counter-sieges, of marches and counter-marches. The Roman Republic could eventually field more than 100,000 men against Hannibal, who saw his forces being consumed by a series of minor and indecisive clashes. By 207 BC, the Carthaginians had been confined to the extreme south of Italy and most of their Italic allies had been defeated by the Romans (including those of Capua, which was reoccupied). While these events took place in Italy, there was some minor fighting in Sicily, where the Carthaginians tried to form an alliance with the powerful Greek city of Syracuse. The Romans besieged Syracuse in 213 BC, and despite using innovative war machines designed by the great engineer and inventor Archimedes, the city was finally captured. The Carthaginians responded by landing an army that occupied several Roman-garrisoned towns in Sicily, but these troops were then crippled by an epidemic and had to refrain from offensive operations. During 211 and 210 BC, the Carthaginian troops in Sicily suffered severe losses and were gradually expelled from their positions. In the spring of 207 BC, Hasdrubal Barca, the brother of Hannibal, marched across the Alps with an army of 30,000 men and tried to join forces with the Carthaginian troops remaining in southern Italy. He and his soldiers, however, were defeated by the Romans at the Battle of the Metaurus, meaning Hannibal could not receive his long-awaited and badly needed reinforcements. In 205 BC, another Carthaginian army landed in north-western Italy under the command of Mago, whose numbers were rapidly expanded by absorbing large numbers of local Ligurian and Celtic allies. Mago, however, was not able to join forces with Hannibal in southern Italy, and was defeated by the Romans at the Battle of Insubria in 203 BC. Soon after these events, Hannibal was forced to leave southern

Italy with his battle-hardened veterans, Publius Cornelius Scipio having invaded Carthaginian North Africa with a large army.

While the military operations described above took place in Italy, the Second Punic War was also fought on a large scale in Iberia. In 218 BC, a Roman army landed in north-eastern Spain and obtained an initial victory over the Carthaginians at the Battle of Cissa. This was followed, in 217 BC, by a naval clash on the Ebro River that ended in success for the Roman fleet. These two Roman successes in Iberia blocked the Carthaginian troops south of the Ebro River and prevented the despatch of reinforcements to Hannibal. In 215 BC, Hasdrubal, as Carthaginian overall commander in Iberia, was soundly defeated by the Romans at the Battle of Dertosa. Following this clash, many Celtiberian communities, which had been loyal allies of the Carthaginians until that moment, changed sides and joined the Romans. In 212 BC, Saguntum was freed by Roman troops, but these were then beaten at the Battle of the Upper Baetis. This defeat was a disaster for the Romans, who were abandoned by the Celtiberians and were forced to fall back on their coastal strongholds north of the Ebro. In 210 BC, Publius Cornelius Scipio arrived in Spain with substantial reinforcements and assumed overall command of the Roman forces there. He captured the most important Carthaginian city of Iberia, New Carthage (modern Cartagena), in 209 BC and started to gain the upper hand in the ongoing military operations. In 208 BC, Hasdrubal and Scipio clashed at the Battle of Baecula, which resulted in an indecisive victory for the Romans. Rallying after their defeat, the Carthaginians were able to move north and cross the Pyrenees with the objective of reaching Italy (where they were defeated, as we have seen, at the Battle of the Metaurus). In 206 BC, at the Battle of Ilipa, Scipio crushed a Carthaginian army that comprised 54,000 warriors and thirty-two war elephants. During the following year, the Carthaginians, under command of Mago, tried to recapture New Carthage but were repulsed. After this failed attempt, Mago went north to cross the Pyrenees and head for Italy (where he was later defeated at Insubria). Following these events, by 204 BC, the whole of Carthaginian Iberia came under Roman control.

After landing in Africa in 204 BC, Scipio was joined by the Numidians of Massinissa. At that time, the two main kingdoms of the Numidians were fighting against each other in a civil war. One of them was ruled by Massinissa, who allied himself with the invading Romans; the other was led by Syphax, who remained loyal to Carthage. The Romans supported Massinissa and the kingdom of Syphax was rapidly occupied by the invaders, who gave it to their new ally. In the autumn of 202 BC, after failed peace negotiations, the Second Punic War was brought to an end by the decisive Battle of Zama. Scipio and his veterans of the fighting in Iberia defeated Hannibal and his veterans of Italy after several hours of bitter fighting. The clash was decided by the superiority of the Roman cavalry (including a substantial number of Numidians) and the failure of an attack by the Carthaginians with their famous war elephants.

The standard panoply of a *triarius*. (*Photo by Diego Casillas and copyright by Divulgación Histórica TANIT*)

After the Battle of Zama, the Romans imposed harsh peace terms on the defeated Carthaginians, according to which Carthage had to renounce all its overseas territories and a good portion of its African possessions. Additionally, the Carthaginians were forbidden from possessing war elephants and from having a fleet of more than ten warships. Finally, they had to pay an immense indemnity of 10,000 silver talents over fifty years and had to send many aristocratic hostages to Rome. In practice, Carthage had lost most of its political autonomy and had to renounce its status as a first-rate power. Following the end of the Second Punic War, Massinissa emerged as the most powerful ruler in North Africa, and for almost fifty years he took advantage of Carthage's military weakness to enlarge his territorial possessions. Rome backed Massinissa's seizures of and raids into Carthaginian lands until 151 BC, when Carthage was finally able to pay off its war indemnity and to raise a new army.

The Carthaginians used their new forces to attack the Numidians of Massinissa, but were decisively defeated by them at the Battle of Oroscopa. During the five decades that followed the Battle of Zama, the Roman Senate was continuously worried about a possible Carthaginian resurgence, especially after the economy of Carthage started to grow again. The Carthaginians had no intention of fighting another war against Rome and sent several diplomatic missions to discuss the situation with the Senate, but Rome nevertheless remained hostile to its old foes. In 149 BC, following the Battle of Oroscopa, the Romans seized the port city of Utica in North Africa and declared war on Carthage with the objective of destroying it once and for all. The Carthaginians sent diplomatic representatives to Utica before the Romans could invade, hoping that a new peace settlement could be reached, but the Romans responded by stating that this was possible only if the Carthaginians handed over all their weapons. Unprepared for war, the Carthaginian government accepted and handed over all its weapons to the invaders, together with the few warships of its fleet. Once Carthage was fully disarmed, the Romans made further demands: the Carthaginians were to abandon their city and relocate it 10 miles away from the sea. At this the Carthaginian representatives abandoned the negotiations and their city started preparing for a long siege. Carthage was well fortified, protected by massive walls, so it was no easy feat for the Romans to besiege it. Two frontal assaults by the Romans were repulsed during the first phase of the siege, while Carthaginian forces harassed the enemy supply lines and foraging parties by conducting fast raids. Carthaginian troops, under command of an experienced commander named Hasdrubal, attacked the Roman camps located outside their city on several occasions and obtained a series of minor victories. The siege became a looser blockade in 148 BC, with the Carthaginians launching further attacks against the Roman positions.

In 147 BC, Scipio Aemilianus – whose adoptive grandfather was Publius Cornelius Scipio, also known as Africanus – was elected consul in Rome and appointed as the overall commander of the legions in Africa. The change of leadership had positive consequences for the Romans, Scipio organizing a successful night attack against Carthage and breaking into the city with a token force of 4,000 men. After having destroyed the suburbs, however, the Romans went back to their camps since they were too few to resist a Carthaginian counter-attack. At this point of the war Scipio built an immense mole to cut off access to Carthage's harbour in an attempt toforce his enemies into starvation. However, the Carthaginians responded by cutting a new channel that connected their harbour to the sea. The Carthaginians were even able to build a new fleet and attack the Roman warships in what became known as the Battle of the Port of Carthage. This ended in a decisive Carthaginian victory. The Romans gained control of the port's quay during the following weeks and constructed a brick structure as high as the Carthaginian walls from which up to 4,000 soldiers could fire onto the city's ramparts from close range. Towards the end of the year, Scipio attacked the main camp of the Carthaginian troops from several directions and overran it, inflicting serious losses. In the spring of 146 BC, the Romans launched a full-scale assault from the harbour area and finally breached the walls of Carthage. For six days the legionaries systematically worked their way through the residential areas of the city, killing everyone they encountered and putting all the buildings to the torch. The siege had been long and bloody, and the Romans were eager to raze Carthage to the ground. At the end of the massacre, during which thousands of civilians were killed,

Roman *triarius* of the manipular legion. (*Photo and copyright by Aera Legio I Consularis*)

Roman *triarius* in defensive position, equipped with long spear and shield. (*Photo and copyright by Aera Legio I Consularis*)

only 50,000 Carthaginians remained alive, all of whom were sold into slavery. The legionaries, meanwhile, pillaged all the city's treasures, and the site was symbolically ploughed to emphasize its annihilation. The Punic Wars had finally come to an end, with the ascendancy of Rome as the dominant military power of the Mediterranean world.

# Chapter 5

# The Macedonian Wars and the Conquest of Greece

The first conflict between the Roman Republic and the Kingdom of Macedonia started in 217 BC, while the Romans were already fighting against the Carthaginians during the Second Punic War. In an attempt to take advantage of the military difficulties Rome was facing with Hannibal's invasion of Italy, the Macedonians decided to attack the Republic while most of its legions were busy fighting Carthage. King Philip V of Macedonia opened hostilities with Rome after its legions had been defeated at the Battle of Lake Trasimene: with Hannibal's Carthaginian army rampaging across Italy, the Macedonian monarch felt sure that the Romans would be unable to oppose his plans for conquering continental Greece and the Illyrian territories of the northern Balkans. During the previous decades, the Roman Republic had, as we have seen, already fought two victorious wars against the Illyrians and its forces had reached the borders of Macedonia. Rome had also gradually obtained naval dominance over the Adriatic Sea. These expansionist moves were unacceptable for the Macedonians, who considered the whole Balkans to be part of their sphere of influence. The First Macedonian War started with a Macedonian invasion of the Illyrian lands on the Adriatic coast. For the first time in their history, the Macedonians built a large fleet with over 100 warships and disembarked their forces in Illyria. The ensuing land campaign, however, was a complete failure for Philip V, who achieved very little. In the summer of 215 BC, after the Romans had been crushed by the Carthaginians at Cannae, the Macedonians sent ambassadors to southern Italy to negotiate a military alliance with Hannibal. The emissaries of Philip V achieved their objectives, but on their return to Macedonia they were captured by the Romans, who learned of the new alliance between Carthage and Macedonia from the official documents they were transporting. In 214 BC, the Macedonian Army tried again to invade Illyria, but the Romans were able to disembark troops on the Balkan coast in order to oppose Philip's new offensive. Despite being few in number, the Roman troops were able to defeat the Macedonians and restore Rome's influence over Illyria. Philip was obliged to abandon his expansionist plans and went back to Macedonian with his army.

During the following years, the Macedonians tried to penetrate into Illyria from the south, while the Romans attempted to conclude a military alliance against Philip with the Aetolian League. The latter was a confederation of Greek communities located on the southern borders of Macedonia which had until recently been at war with Philip. The Aetolians concluded an alliance with Rome in 211 BC in order to fight more effectively against the common enemy, Macedonia. During the following year, the Hellenistic Kingdom of Pergamon also joined the anti-Macedonian alliance and sent its fleet to the Adriatic in order to support the Romans. The Macedonians had destroyed their own fleet after their first failed invasion of Illyria so it would not fall into Roman hands, meaning the allies were able to control the Adriatic without any opposition. The Macedonians fought in mainland Greece against the Aetolians over the following years, obtaining the support of the Achaean League (another confederation of Greek communities and the mortal enemy of the Aetolian League). In 206 BC, after having suffered several considerable defeats, the Aetolians made peace with Philip. The Aetolians' Roman allies had been heavily involved in the campaigns against Carthage and thus could not offer any substantial help, while the fleet of Pergamon had returned to Anatolia so the Aetolians had been left without any allies. The First Macedonian War officially came to an end in 205 BC with the signing of the Treaty of Phoenice, according to which Philip V renounced his alliance with Carthage but could exert direct influence over some areas of Illyria. In practice, very little had changed from the situation in 217 BC. However, it was clear that Rome and Macedonia would fight a new war for dominance over the Balkans as soon as Hannibal was defeated (which happened in 202 BC with the Roman victory at Zama).

The Second Macedonian War broke out in 200 BC after Philip V invaded Attica and menaced the city of Athens. Advancing from their bases in Illyria, the Romans attacked Macedonia from the west but were unable to secure a clear victory. The Roman Republic was again joined in the struggle by the Kingdom of Pergamon and the Aetolian League, Pergamon sending its fleet and the League attacking Macedonia from the south. In 198 BC, after several months of inconclusive operations, the Romans landed in the Balkans with a substantial army. The Roman expeditionary force was able to achieve a victory in Epirus, at the Battle of the Aous River, but the clash was not decisive. Meanwhile, at sea, the allied fleet of Rome and Pergamon reinforced Athens, which convinced the Achaean League to join the anti-Macedonian alliance. During the winter of 198/197 BC, the opposing sides tried to find a compromise in order to bring hostilities to an end, but the peace negotiations came to nothing. The decisive clash of the Second Macedonian War was fought at Cynoscephalae in 197 BC. Here, for the first time on Greek soil, the Macedonian phalanx faced the Roman legions, with 26,000 Romans emerging victorious against 25,000 Macedonians. The battle took place on hilly terrain, where Philip's heavy infantry did not have the space to manoeuvre properly. This greatly advantaged the flexible Roman legions, which

Roman legionary of Sulla's army. (*Photo and copyright by Aera Legio I Consularis*)

resisted the enemy charge and then used their missile weapons in deadly fashion. After this defeat, having also suffered significant losses on other secondary fronts, the Macedonian king decided to make peace with Rome. The Macedonians were forced to remove all their garrisons that were scattered across Greece, and, for the first time since the age of Philip II, they were obliged to acknowledge the political freedom of the Greek cities. Philip V also had to pay a large war indemnity and was forced to surrender all his naval forces. Macedonia's army, meanwhile, was reduced to just 5,000 soldiers and was officially forbidden to have war elephants. Thanks to its victory in the Second Macedonian War, Rome could present itself as the saviour of Greek freedom: however, it had simply replaced Macedon's predominance over Greece with its own.

After the Second Macedonian War, the Roman Republic started to intervene quite frequently in Greece, taking advantage of the Macedonians' temporary military weakness and of the Greeks' political divisions. The various small states of Greece were organized into two major military leagues that almost constantly fought against each other: the Achaean League and the Aetolian League. The Achaean League had been created by the Macedonians almost two centuries before and had long been dominated by them, whereas the Aetolian League, albeit smaller and weaker, had always opposed the political ambitions of Macedonia. In addition to these two leagues there was the city of Sparta, which while declining as a major military power was still autonomous and ambitious. During the Second Macedonian War, the Spartans and their ambitious monarch Nabis sided with the Macedonians, hoping to gain some territorial advantage. Indeed, they were given the city of Argos, located in the northern Peloponnese, in exchange for fighting against the Romans. When the conflict turned against Macedonia, however, the Spartans changed sides and allied themselves with Rome in an attempt to retain control over Argos. After the end of hostilities, Rome did not restore the independence of Argos, the Republic seeking to have Sparta as a regional ally. During the following years, however, Nabis tried to restore the ancient military power of Sparta: he confiscated large amounts of property from the wealthiest citizens of his state and distributed them to new owners, who paid him with substantial sums of money. This wealth was used to engage thousands of mercenaries and to liberate many slaves (helots) who soon became extremely loyal to Nabis. The Spartan king also turned the port of Gythium into a major naval arsenal and fortified the city of Sparta. He formed strong military alliances with the rulers of Crete, who provided him with substantial numbers of mercenaries (mostly archers). Coming under strong pressure from the Achaean League – which could not tolerate the occupation of one of its members, Argos – and fearing a resurgence of Sparta's military power, the Romans organized a council of the Greek states that

Roman legionary with Montefortino helmet. (*Photo and copyright by Aera Legio I Consularis*)

took place at Corinth in 195 BC. All the Greeks, with the exception of the Aetolian League and of Thessaly, declared their readiness to help Rome wage war on Sparta.

An army of 40,000 Romans and Greeks advanced towards the Peloponnese after Nabis refused to come to terms. Instead of besieging Argos, as expected by most of the Greeks, the Romans moved south to invade Laconia, the homeland of the Spartans. Nabis could count on an army of 10,000 citizens (mostly freed slaves), 3,000 mercenaries and 2,000 Cretan allies. After some minor skirmishes, which saw the Romans prevailing, the Spartans refused to give battle on the open field and retreated into their city. The Romans and Greeks plundered Sparta's countryside before besieging the port of Gythium. The port's garrison eventually surrendered, but was permitted to return – unharmed – to Sparta. After some failed peace negotiations, the allied force besieged Sparta with an army of 50,000 men. Nabis came out from his city before being completely surrounded, but was defeated in battle. The Romans did not want a prolonged siege of the city, so immediately attempted to storm it. The ensuing clash on Sparta's walls was extremely violent and continued in the narrow streets of the city. Nabis, seeing that his defences were collapsing, tried to flee but was forced to surrender after most of Sparta was destroyed by fire. Meanwhile, upon hearing that Sparta was under attack, the citizens of Argos revolted against the Spartan garrison of their city and forced it to return to Sparta. With the end of hostilities, Argos regained its former independence and was readmitted into the Achaean League. Nabis remained on the Spartan throne, but had to renounce all his naval bases. However, soon after the Romans left Greece, the Spartan monarch started to build a new fleet and to raise a fresh army with the support of the Aetolian League. The Achaean League responded by inviting the Romans to return and sending an expedition against Gythium. The venture was a complete failure, but the Achaeans were able to ravage Laconia for a month without encountering any opposition. At this point, understanding that Nabis was too weak to confront a Roman force which had just landed in Greece, the Aetolians abandoned their ally and killed him. The Achaean forces occupied Sparta without having to fight and forced it to become a member of their league.

Within a few years Sparta ceased to be a regional military power in the Peloponnese, not being permitted to have any city walls (those built by Nabis were demolished) or a fleet of warships. The Aetolian League benefited greatly from this and became the main anti-Roman power of Greece, in contrast to the Achaean League that was strongly pro-Roman. The Aetolians understood that they had no chance of defeating the Romans alone, and thus gradually formed a military alliance with the Seleucid Empire, the most important Hellenistic power of Asia. The Seleucids, after the end of the Second Punic War, had welcomed Hannibal as a political exile

Roman legionary of the civil wars. (*Photo and copyright by Aera Legio I Consularis*)

and had gradually adopted a strong anti-Roman diplomatic position. Antiochus III, ruler of the Seleucid Empire, was finally convinced by Hannibal (who became his main military advisor) and the Aetolians to invade Greece with his troops in order to use the growing anti-Roman sentiment of the Greeks to his advantage. The Seleucids crossed the Hellespont with an army of 10,000 infantry, 500 cavalry and six war elephants. The Achaean League remained loyal to the Romans, but could do little to stop the Seleucid advance across eastern Greece before the arrival of the Roman legions. Antiochus III tried to form an alliance with the Kingdom of Macedonia, but it remained loyal to the Romans. During the winter of 192/191 BC, the Seleucids occupied most of Thessaly, while the Romans landed a large army in Illyria, comprising 20,000 infantry, 2,000 mounted troops and fifteen war elephants. The Romans already had 16,000 legionaries and allied soldiers in Greece, so they significantly outnumbered the Seleucids. Soon after the arrival of the Roman expeditionary force, the Seleucid troops started to experience serious difficulties: they were expelled from Thessaly by the Macedonians and did not receive the expected substantial reinforcements from their Aetolian allies (who feared that their homeland could be invaded by the Romans). As a result, Anthiochus III withdrew to the Thermopylae Pass, where he attempted to stop the advancing Romans. The Seleucids built strong defensive positions in the pass – scene of the heroic Spartan stand against Persian invaders almost 300 years previously – in the hope of defending it until the arrival of massive reinforcements from Asia. An opening frontal assault by the Romans was repulsed with heavy casualties, but the attackers continued to press on against the Seleucid phalangites deployed in the pass. The Romans were in the end able to conduct an effective outflanking manoeuvre and invested the Seleucid camp located to the rear of their enemies' main positions. The phalangites, taken by surprise, soon abandoned their positions and fled the pass in complete disarray. After this defeat, Antiochus III was forced to abandon Greece, only for the Romans – under the command of Scipio Asiaticus – to follow him and invade Asia Minor.

In order to cross the Hellespont, the Romans had to secure their control over the Aegean Sea, for which they sent their fleet against that of the Seleucids. The Romans could count on the support of the Rhodian warships, Rhodes being one of their most important allies together with the Hellenistic Kingdom of Pergamon. Polyxenidas, the overall commander of the Seleucid fleet, was first defeated by a Roman and Pergamene fleet at the Battle of Corycus in 191 BC, then crushed by a Roman and Rhodian fleet at the Battle of Myonessus the following year. After landing in Asia Minor, the Romans faced a large Seleucid army consisting of 60,000 men with fifty-four war elephants. The decisive pitched battle of the conflict was fought at Magnesia in late 190 BC. The clash took place on a horseshoe-shaped plain, where the Seleucids could deploy their heavily armoured cataphract cavalry, who were supported by a sizeable number of scythed chariots. The battle began with an attack of the Pargamene light infantry, who routed the Seleucid scythed chariots, which panicked and fled from the battlefield, causing confusion among the cataphracts positioned behind them. The Roman cavalry took advantage of this and broke through the enemy left flank, meaning the Seleucid phalanx, which was deployed in the centre, came under attack from its front and left side. Coming under heavy missile fire from light troops, the Seleucid phalanx lost cohesion and abandoned the battlefield. The Battle of Magnesia was a disaster for the Seleucids, who lost around 15,000 men. In 189 BC, the bloody conflict between the Roman Republic and the Seleucid Empire came to an end. The Seleucids were forced to renounce all their claims on lands located west of the Taurus Mountains (i.e. Anatolia) and had to pay a heavy war indemnity to the Romans.

Under the terms of the peace treaty, the Seleucids also had to hand over Hannibal to the Republic, but the great Carthaginian warlord fled to the Hellenistic Kingdom of Bithynia before he could be captured by the Romans. Hannibal eventually died in 181 BC, committing suicide after learning that a Roman embassy had been sent to Bithynia to capture him. The Treaty of Apamea that ended the Roman–Seleucid War had very positive results for Rome's allies: Rhodes obtained Lycia and Caria in Anatolia, while the Kingdom of Pergamon received part of Thrace and most of the Anatolian lands west of the Taurus Mountains. The once mighty Seleucid fleet was reduced to just ten warships, thereby conceding full control over the Aegean to Rome. While fighting against the Seleucids in Asia, the Romans also conducted a parallel war against the Aetolian League in Greece. The Aetolians had been abandoned by their Seleucid allies, but fought hard to defend their homeland. An invading Roman force besieged the city of Naupactus for two months, but was unable to capture it. Meanwhile, the Aetolians seized the mountain pass at Mount Corax and prepared for a desperate resistance. After further indecisive fighting, which saw the arrival of troops from the Achaean League, the Aetolians made peace with the Romans and formed an alliance with them. Following their victory at Magnesia, the Romans started to indirectly control Anatolia by supporting the expansionist ambitions of the Kingdom of Pergamon, which had long wanted to invade Galatia, a kingdom that had been created by the migrating Celts in the heart of Anatolia several decades before. The Galatians had become rich from plundering the small Hellenistic states on the borders of their realm, and thus represented a menace for the political stability of Anatolia. A combined Roman and Pergamene army invaded Galatia in 189 BC. In early skirmishing near Cuballum, a force of Galatian cavalry that had attacked the invaders was defeated. The Romans and Pergamese reached the enemy capital

Roman legionary of the civil wars. (*Photo and copyright by Aera Legio I Consularis*)

of Gordium, seizing it without a fight. The Galatians held a fortified position on the nearby Mount Olympus, where they awaited the Romans. The Galatian troops defended their positions with great determination during the ensuing fight, but all were massacred. The decisive battle of the Roman–Galatian War took place at Ancyra, where the Galatians were utterly defeated. After having suffered two disastrous defeats, they sued for peace. The Kingdom of Galatia was then deprived of all its treasures and became a Pergamene protectorate.

Philip V died in 179 BC, his ambitious son, Perseus, then becoming King of Macedonia. Perseus had great plans for the expansion of his realm and the restoration of the ancient glory of Macedon. To achieve this goal, he spent most of his early reign trying to form a large anti-Roman alliance that comprised the Seleucid Empire as well as many of the Greek cities, who had soon started to hate the Romans after the Republic assumed indirect control of their territories. The Third Macedonian War broke out in 171 BC, in which the Romans were supported by their allies of the Aetolian League and Pontus. While the Roman Army disembarked in Greece, the Macedonian military forces invaded Thessaly from the north. Thessaly had been part of the Macedonian realm since it was conquered by Philip II, and Perseus was eager to bring it back under the influence of Macedon. It was in Thessaly that the first significant clash of the Third Macedonian War was fought, at Callinicus. This ended in a significant victory for Perseus, who defeated the Romans thanks to the superiority of his cavalry and light infantry. The war, however, continued. In 169 BC, the Macedonians invaded Illyria, having secured their homeland from attack by Thessaly. The invasion was a success, Perseus' forces conquering many Illyrian strongholds and capturing over 1,500 soldiers of the Roman garrisons. During the winter of the same year, the Macedonians also invaded Aetolia, but this operation ended without significant results. In the following spring, the Romans landed an army in Epirus and marched on Macedonia, but had to face a strong resistance during their advance through the mountains. Perseus' light infantry fought with great distinction during these clashes, slowing down the movement of the Roman legions. Consequently, the Romans were not able to invade Macedonia as they had planned. The decisive year of the war was 168 BC, with a major pitched battle being fought north of Thessaly at Pydna.

The Battle of Pydna was one of the most important clashes of Antiquity. Perseus deployed his whole military potential, with 39,000 infantry and 4,000 cavalry facing a Roman army of 36,000 infantry and 2,600 cavalry. By the time the battle had ended, Perseus had lost most of his forces, with some 11,000 of his troops captured by the Romans. The Macedonian military potential had been broken forever. After the defeat, Perseus retreated north to his capital of Pella with what remained of his cavalry.

Roman legionary of the civil wars. (*Photo and copyright by Aera Legio I Consularis*)

Despite having suffered severe losses, he was determined to continue his resistance. However, the young Macedonian monarch was soon surrounded by Roman forces and had no choice but to surrender. After being captured, he was sent in chains to Rome, where he spent the rest of his life in captivity. With the Third Macedonian War over, Rome was determined to avoid any future resurgence by Macedonia. The Senate decided to break up the Kingdom of Macedonia into four separate Roman protectorates. Rome exerted control over all the natural resources of the country, in particular the gold and silver mines, and Macedonia was garrisoned by Roman troops. The harsh peace conditions imposed by the Roman Republic were resented by the Macedonians, who were forced to become vassals of a foreign power after having been the dominant state of the Greek world for two centuries. In 150 BC, a man named Andriscus, pretending to be a son of King Perseus, led a popular uprising in the four cantons of Macedonia. The rebellion soon spread, leading to the Fourth Macedonian War. Despite having few soldiers under his command, Andriscus was able to obtain several victories and thus his uprising continued until 148 BC, when the Romans were finally able to restore order in Macedonia by using harsh repressive methods.

With the Roman victory in the Fourth Macedonian War it became apparent that Greece was going to lose any form of real independence. As a result, two opposing factions emerged inside the Achaean League: one called for Greece to determine its own foreign policy in an autonomous way, while the other believed that Greece should submit to Rome in order to have peace and prosperity. In 146 BC, while fighting against Carthage in North Africa, the Roman Republic decided to reduce the number of Greek states admitted to the Achaean League in order to weaken the military alliance. The Greeks, outraged by this move, declared war on Rome, electing Critolaos as overall commander of the Achaean League's forces. Nevertheless, the Achaean War went Rome's way from the beginning, Critolaos' forces being defeated at the Battle of Scarpheia and the Greek leader thereafter committing suicide. This military disaster pushed the Achaean League into trying to make peace with the Roman Republic, but the negotiations came to nothing. Hostilities thus continued, with the remaining troops of the Achaean League gathered in its capital of Corinth. A 26,000-strong Roman army besieged the city, which was defended by 14,000 Greeks. The Greeks came out from behind Corinth's walls to attack the Romans, but were completely routed in battle. After three days of fighting in the city, the legionaries were finally able to occupy Corinth. The entire adult male population of the city was massacred, while all the women and children were enslaved. The city was razed to the ground, an act that terrorized all the Greeks. Following the fall of Corinth, all the military leagues of Greece were dissolved and the whole country came under direct Roman control.

Thracian warrior equipped as a 'peltast' light infantryman. (*Photo and copyright by Ancient Thrace*)

The Macedonian Wars also had a deep impact on the destiny of the Thracians, whose participation in the four conflicts had been quite significant. During the Second Macedonian War, for example, some 2,000 Thracian warriors were part of the Macedonian army that fought at the Battle of Cynocephalae in 197 BC. With the end of the hostilities in 196 BC, the Thracians were freed from any form of indirect Macedonian rule. The various Thracian tribes, however, became increasingly worried by the expanding Roman military presence in the Balkans. With the defeat of Macedonia, a significant power vacuum had been created in Greece: the Romans wanted to fill this with their own legions, but the Seleucid Empire was also keen to conquer this southern portion of the Balkans. As we have seen, in 192 BC, hostilities commenced between the Roman Republic and the Seleucid Empire. Two years after the outbreak of the war, the Romans obtained a decisive victory over their Seleucid opponents at the Battle of Magnesia in Anatolia. While returning back to Greece, however, the victorious Roman troops were attacked by Thracians forces. Thrace had assembled an army of 10,000 warriors and waited for the Romans at a narrow forest pass in south-eastern Thrace. The tribal fighters attacked the Roman rearguard, which comprised a baggage train full of riches that had been taken from the defeated Seleucids. The Romans were taken by surprise and routed, all their wagons being looted before the Thracians retired to their forests after seeing upcoming Roman reinforcements. This little-known ambush was a disaster for the Romans, one they would never forget. Although it had been a success for the Thracians, it was obviously not a decisive one for the destiny of the country. Upon the outbreak of the Third Macedonian War, Perseus' armies contained around 3,000 Thracians, who were later supplemented by another 2,000 fighters provided by the Odrysian tribe, which was an ally of Macedonia. At the Battle of Callinicus in 171 BC, the Thracians fighting with the Macedonians obtained a clear victory over the Romans: according to ancient sources they returned from the battlefield singing and with hundreds of severed Roman heads. This was the second time that the Thracians had humiliated the Romans, but the Thracian success could not stop the expansion of the Roman Republic. In 168 BC, the Macedonian Army was soundly defeated by Rome at the Battle of Pydna, which practically ended the Third Macedonian War and transformed the Macedonians into Roman vassals. At this point the Thracians found themselves with the Roman legions at their frontiers.

In 150 BC – as we have seen – an attempt to re-establish an independent Kingdom of Macedonia provoked the outbreak of the Fourth Macedonian War, which lasted until 148 BC. The Thracians were once again part of the anti-Roman alliance, but the pretender to the Macedonian throne was defeated by the Republic and in 146 BC Macedonia was officially transformed into a Roman province. A constant state of war

Roman legionary standing outside his tent. (*Photo and copyright by Aera Legio I Consularis*)

thereafter existed on the border between Roman Macedonia and independent Thrace, with Rome wanting to transform the various Thracian tribes into client communities since they considered themselves the heirs of Macedonia's political influence over Thrace. The Thracians had no intention of accepting the Romans as their overlords, soon starting to launch aggressive raids against the province of Macedonia. Roman armies were defeated on several occasions during the many small-scale wars fought

Thracian warrior equipped with sword and shield. (*Photo and copyright by Ancient Thrace*)

Thracian warrior armed with curved knife. (*Photo and copyright by Ancient Thrace*)

against the Thracians, even having one their proconsuls killed. The Thracian warriors, with their elusive skirmishing tactics and great mobility, proved very difficult for the Romans to defeat, the legionaries knowing little of the Balkan territory on which they fought. From 146 BC, the Roman Republic tried to create some sort of unified Thracian state in order to transform the territory into one of its vassal kingdoms, it being much easier for Rome to control a single puppet kingdom than keep order among many warlike tribes. Around 100 BC, a new Odrysian Kingdom was established, but this did not last long due to the internal divisions of the Thracians, most of whom were strongly against Rome's indirect rule of their homeland. By about 30 BC, some form of Thracian Kingdom had been restored by the Romans, by which time all the Thracian tribes, even those that were still autonomous, had accepted some form of Roman suzerainty.

## Chapter 6

# The Conquest of Iberia and the Jugurthine War

Ancient Iberia was inhabited by two main ethnic groups: in the west and the centre of the peninsula there were the fierce communities of Celtiberians, while in the east there were the powerful Iberian tribes. Since 575 BC, the Carthaginians had started to create commercial colonies on the southern and eastern coast of Spain, but these exerted only a limited influence over the local populations. This situation changed completely with the outbreak of the Punic Wars. Carthage, unlike Rome, could count on few human and natural resources because the territory of North Africa was not as rich as that of Italy. As a result, the Carthaginians badly needed new lands from which they could take natural resources (such as minerals or metals) and recruit large numbers of expert soldiers. Iberia was their natural choice: ancient Spain was extremely rich of mineral resources, especially gold and silver, while the local tribes were well known in the Mediterranean world for the deadly skills of their warriors. The Iberian slingers from the Balearic Islands, for example, served as mercenaries in most armies of the time, and were considered elite troops by those who employed them. The Iberians, similarly to the Celts, produced magnificent weapons, which were exported around the entire Mediterranean world and influenced the combat techniques of both the Carthaginians and the Romans. Two weapons, in particular, became iconic of the Iberian warriors: the *falcata* (a sword with a single-edged blade that pitches forward towards the point) and the *gladius* (a short stabbing sword, used to strike with the point). The latter became the standard sword of the Roman infantry, being adopted by the legions after the Republic fought against the Iberians. Spanish armies of the time included excellent contingents of heavy infantry and cavalry, but also deadly light skirmishers. The Carthaginians understood that by using such a great military potential they would be able to face the Roman legions. Consequently, after its defeat in the First Punic War, Carthage sent its best general – Hamilcar Barca, father of Hannibal – to submit Iberia. After eight years of campaigning, by using his mastery in both force of arms and diplomacy, Hamilcar was able to conquer most of central and eastern Iberia. The local tribes accepted Carthaginian supremacy, but in most cases they retained a high degree of autonomy. The Carthaginians thus received permission to exploit the natural resources of their territory, but could not interfere with the

Roman legionary of the early Empire equipped with *dolabra* pickaxe. (*Photo and copyright by Legio XIII Gemina*)

Working tools employed by the Roman legionaries. (*Photo and copyright by Legio XIII Gemina*)

region's internal politics. In case of war, the Iberians were to provide large military contingents to Carthage. These could be made up of allies or mercenaries, and formed the largest part of Carthage's army.

During the Second Punic War, understanding that Carthage's power was based on the resources of Iberia, the Romans sent various generals and armies to Spain in order to expel the Carthaginians from the region. After several bloody battles, by the end of the conflict, the Romans were able to conquer and occupy all the Iberian lands that had been under Carthaginian control. The local tribes, however, continued to revolt against the Republic for many decades. As we have seen, Punic control of Iberia had not been very strict, but that of Rome was completely different. During their rebellions against Roman control, the Iberians were helped by the Celtiberians of western Spain, who had remained independent from both Carthage and Rome. As a result, the Romans soon realized that the only way to pacify Spain was to also conquer the lands of the Celtiberians. This, however, proved an extremely difficult proposition, as the Celtiberians were masters of guerrilla warfare and had intimate knowledge of their mountain territory. The first Roman military operations against the Celtiberians started as early as 197 BC, just a few years after the end of the Second Punic War. From the beginning, their military operations in Spain were characterized by a series of crushing defeats for the Romans. In 181 BC, the first of two Celtiberian Wars broke out in Spain, ending in 179 BC when Tiberius Gracchus signed peace treaties with most of the Celtiberian leaders. As the Romans had not been able to pacify the Celtiberian lands, the treaties were quite favourable for the Celts of Spain, who retained complete control over their lands but in exchange had to provide allied military contingents and large amounts of grain to Rome. After more than two decades of relative peace in Iberia, the Second Celtiberian War broke out in 154 BC. This conflict lasted for two years and included a series of great Celtiberian victories. In order to eventually prevail, the Romans had to use very harsh methods, fighting with great violence and committing a series of abuses against the civilian population. By 151 BC, it seemed that the Celtiberians had finally been defeated by Rome, albeit they were still in control of most of their lands. In 155 BC, the Iberian tribes of southern Spain had launched a general revolt against the Romans which continued for many years. This was guided by their great military leader Viriathus and became known as the Lusitanian War (from the name of Viriathus' tribe, the main driving force of the rebellion). The Celtiberians broke their pacts with Rome in 144 BC and joined the revolt of Viriathus. For the first time, most of the Iberian and Celtiberian tribes were now united in pursuit of a common objective. Viriathus' aim was to expel the Romans from all Iberian territories, and his war lasted for more than fifteen years, ending only in 139 BC. During that period, the Romans were on the verge of losing Spain on several occasions, but Viriathus was eventually assassinated and the rebels were then crushed. Iberia thereafter became the Roman Hispania and the Republic dominated much of present-day Spain and Portugal. Most of the Celtiberian lands were occupied, with the exception of some small territories in north-western Spain, where, in present-day Cantabria and Asturias, two tribes continued to resist by using irregular warfare tactics. The area was extremely marginal from an economic point of view, being entirely covered with mountains and located on the western edge of the Roman-held lands, so the Cantabri and Astures were able to retain their independence until the reign of Augustus.

After the end of the Third Punic War and with the destruction of Carthage, Rome gained an important foothold in North Africa and could create a new province in the former Carthaginian lands. The Kingdom of Numidia, which had been one of Carthage's main allies during the Second Punic War but had changed sides during the Third Punic War, remained fully independent after 146 BC and established a very positive relationship with the Republic. Territorially it comprised the Mediterranean coastline of present-day Algeria and thus bordered with the new Roman territorial possessions in Tunisia. In 149 BC, the great king of the Numidians, Massinissa, died and was succeeded by his son, Micipsa, who ruled Numidia as a loyal ally of Rome until 118 BC. The Numidians were famous across the Mediterranean world for the great combat capabilities of their warriors, who were skilled light cavalrymen and light infantrymen. Armed with light javelins specifically designed for throwing, the Numidians were masters in organizing ambushes and were capable of moving rapidly on every kind of terrain. Living on the outskirts of the desert, they knew how to conduct long-range scouting operations and to skirmish from a distance with enemies deploying superior military forces. The Numidians had long been a fundamental component of the Carthaginian armies and had been one of the key elements behind Hannibal's victories. They collaborated with the Romans on several occasions during the long reign of Micipsa, providing them with excellent contingents of mounted auxiliaries. When Micipsa died, there were three potential heirs to the Numidian throne: two of his sons (Adherbal and Hiempsal) and an illegitimate nephew of the king named Jugurtha. The latter had fought with the Romans in Iberia for many years and had learned a lot there about Roman warfare. Micipsa, fearing that upon his death Jugurtha could usurp the Numidia from his sons with the help of the Romans, adopted him. In 118 BC, the three heirs to the Numidian throne, with the support of Rome, decided to divide Numidia into three separate kingdoms in order to avoid the outbreak of civil wars. Soon, however, the ambitious Jugurtha declared war on his cousins: Hiempsal was assassinated by Jugurtha's men, while Adherbal was defeated and forced to leave Numidia. Adherbal fled to Rome, where he appealed for arbitration to the Senate. The Romans, being sure of Jugurtha's loyalty towards the Republic, were quite happy about the possibility of having a single Kingdom of Numidia ruled by their ally. However, they were forced to organize a commission tasked with dividing Numidia into two parts between the pretenders to the throne.

Jugurtha, thanks to his personal connections in Rome, bribed the Roman officials of the commission to assign him the more fertile and populous western half of Numidia. Adherbal had no option but to accept what had been decided by the commission and made peace with his cousin. In 113 BC, however, Jugurtha attacked Adherbal and defeated his forces, after which the few warriors still supporting Adherbal were besieged in the city of Cirta. The Romans tried to end the conflict by sending a new commission to Numidia, but this returned to Rome without achieving anything and Cirta was finally conquered by Jugurtha. Soon after, Jugurtha ordered the execution of his cousin and all private Roman citizens (mostly merchants) who had supported Adherbal during the defence of Cirta. The Roman Republic declared war on Jugurtha in 111 BC, with Lucius Calpurnius Bestia, consul for the year, being appointed overall commander of the Roman forces in Africa. He soon concluded an alliance with Bocchus, the monarch of the Kingdom of Mauretania, located on the coastline of present-day Morocco and a fierce regional rival of Numidia. Bocchus was the father-in-law of Jugurtha but hated his young relative. Before hostilities could commence, however, the Senate of Rome was again bribed by Jugurtha and decided to suspend the war by offering lenient terms to Numidia. Jugurtha was required to pay only a small fine for his crimes and was asked to give his war elephants to the Romans. The corruption of the Senate led to popular outcry in Rome, people being angry that the institutions of the Republic seemed to be on the verge of collapse if an enemy could 'defeat' the Romans with money.

To stop the protests of the people, the Senate organized a formal investigation and Jugurtha was summoned to Rome to appear as a witness. However, he bribed two tribunes and was prevented from testifying. Before leaving the city, Jugurtha even organized the assassination of one of his relatives who had claims to the Numidian throne and who lived in Rome. The Senate was ultimately compelled by the fury of the citizens to revoke the peace treaty that had been signed with Numidia and to once again declare war on Jugurtha. The consul Spurius Postumius Albinus took command of the Roman forces in Africa but failed to carry out energetic action, later leaving the direction of military operations to his brother, Aulus Postumius Albinus. Aulus attacked the city of Suthul, where the Numidian treasury was kept, but failed to capture it due to the strong resistance of the garrison. Jugurtha then lured the Romans into the desolate wilds of the Sahara Desert and attacked them with effective hit-and-run tactics, causing serious losses. An entire Roman army was eventually forced to surrender and to pass under the yoke, a humiliation that the Romans had only previously experienced during the Samnite Wars more than 200 years previously. Following this disaster, Quintus Metellus, a plebeian with a reputation for integrity and courage, was nominated as commander of the Roman army in Africa. Metellus restored discipline and organization in the ranks of the Roman troops and was able to obtain a victory over Jugurtha at the Battle of the Muthul. The Numidian king, however, evaded capture.

After the failure of peace negotiations, Jugurtha dismissed most of his low-quality recruits and continued the conflict by using guerrilla tactics with only his best troops. Metellus captured several Numidian cities and tried to provoke Jugurtha to fight another pitched battle. The Romans were finally able to intercept the Numidians, but Jugurtha fled to the fortress of Thala. Located deep in the desert, Thala was accessible only after an excruciating three-day march across the desert without any water sources. Nevertheleess, the Romans were able to capture Thala after a siege of forty days, but Jugurtha once again managed to escape. Metellus was then replaced as overall commander by his young lieutenant, Gaius Marius, who had already demonstrated himself an excellent military leader. In 107 BC, Marius plundered most of the Numidian countryside and used harsh methods to submit the local communities. Meanwhile, Bocchus of Mauretania had decided to ally himself with Jugurtha, fearing that the Romans could also occupy his kingdom. The joint forces of

Jugurtha and Bocchus, mostly consisting of excellent light cavalry, attacked Marius' legionaries on the open field but the clash ended in a Roman defensive victory. At this point of the conflict Bocchus abandoned his ally and handed Jugurtha to the Romans after having massacred the Numidian troops. The Jugurthine War had finally come to an end, the Numidian monarch being imprisoned in Rome where he died in 104 BC, his realm being divided between the Romans and Bocchus. The Kingdom of Mauretania, following Bocchus' death in 80 BC, progressively became a Roman client state and was finally organized as a Roman province in AD 44. The long African conflict clearly revealed the many problems that the late Roman Republic was experiencing: in particular, leading Romans now sought individual power at the expense of the state and thus were open to bribery. A moral and ethical decline was taking place in Rome, and corruption was widespread. The era of the civil wars was on the horizon, and two Roman generals who had fought with distinction in the Jugurthine War would initiate it: Gaius Marius and Lucius Cornelius Sulla.

# Chapter 7

# The Cimbrian War and Marius' Military Reform

Around 150 BC, a demographic explosion occurred in southern Scandinavia, causing a rapid expansion of the population that was not sustainable for the natural resources of northern Europe. As a result, two of the most important Germanic tribes that were settled in the Jutland Peninsula migrated south in search of new lands where they could live. These tribes were the Cimbri and Teutones. During the previous decades, the Germanic communities had intensified their commercial exchanges with the Celts, from whom they learned something about the rich southern lands that were dominated by the Romans. The regions located around the Mediterranean had a warm, sunny climate and were perfect for agriculture, being characterized by the presence of important natural resources as well as the existence of large urban centres inhabited by thousands of citizens. These southern lands would be a perfect new homeland for the Germani, who could no longer survive in northern Europe due to a serious lack of food. Feeling they had no other choice, the warlike Cimbri and Teutones moved south and crossed Germany in search of new lands. They migrated with their families and all their goods: they truly were peoples on the move, a Germanic tradition that would continue until well after the fall of the Roman Empire. This massive migration was an unknown phenomenon at the time, with many thousands of people pushing against the northern frontier of the Roman Republic in the hope of a better life. The Romans had never experienced anything like it and were ill-prepared to deal with the situation.

On the north-eastern frontier of the Italian peninsula, bordering with present-day Austria, the Romans had organized a buffer zone for protection of the Republic: this was not a province, but rather a client state known as the Kingdom of Noricum. It was originally inhabited by several Celtic tribes, which were gradually unified into a federal state under the strong influence of Rome. The Celts of Noricum had strong political and commercial relations with those living in Pannonia (modern Hungary) and the other Celtic tribes settled in Switzerland. Noricum was in a delicate geographical position, with Roman Italy to the south and the fierce Germanic 'nations' to the north. Its political leaders therefore had no choice but to form an alliance with the Roman Republic in order to obtain military protection. The Kingdom of Noricum had been created around 150 BC, and from the outset

Germanic warrior armed with club. (*Photo and copyright by Ancient Thrace*)

Roman legionary of the early Empire, with the new rectangular shield. (*Photo and copyright by Legio XIII Gemina*)

it provided the Romans with large amounts of well-made weapons. Celtic Austria was famed for the high quality production of metal weapons and tools. Noricum was rich in deposits of iron, gold and salt, natural resources that both the Romans and the Germani badly needed, so the local Celts had to maintain some kind of equilibrium in order to preserve their independence. Noric steel was particularly appreciated for its quality and hardness: most of the weapons used to equip the Roman legions were manufactured from it. Between Provence (modern south-east France) and Noricum, in present-day Switzerland, the political situation was quite different, the Celts living not enjoying positive relations with Rome. By the second century BC, the Swiss plateau was entirely occupied by the Helvetii, who lived on territory that was full of natural resources, especially of gold (which could be easily found in many rivers, not only underground in mines). The Helvetii were not a single tribe, but a confederation of four groups, having apparently originally lived in southern Germany. Around 150 BC, under strong pressure from the Germanic tribes to the north, they had to move south and settle in the Alpine area. It appears that both the confederation of the Helvetii and the Kingdom of Noricum were formed around the middle of the second century BC as a result of the mass migrations of the Cimbri and Teutones.

Before reaching the Danube and the Kingdom of Noricum, the Cimbri and Teutones encountered and defeated the Scordisci during their march south. The Scordisci were a Celtic tribe originally settled in present-day Hungary, who had participated in the great Celtic 'invasion' of the Balkans that saw the sacking of Greece. During their march home after the end of that expedition, the Scordisci decided to stop at the mouth of the River Sava and to establish new settlements there. Philip V of Macedonia developed a very good relationship with them, since he wanted to employ these Celts as allies against the Illyrian and Thracian tribes and against Rome. The Scordisci soon became a significant regional power in the central Balkans, building two fortresses to protect their new homeland and submitting several of the local tribes. After the transformation of Macedonia into a Roman province (146 BC), the Scordisci were constantly at war against Rome and launched frequent incursions into its territory. In 135 BC, the Romans obtained their first victory over the Scordisci, after which part of the tribe moved north, settling on the eastern borders of Noricum and Pannonia. These refugees were crushed by the Germani moving from the north, and most of their survivors joined the Cimbri and the Teutones in their attack on Noricum. The Taurisci were the first Celtic tribe of Noricum to be invested by the newcomers, who were incredibly powerful from a military point of view. The warriors of the Cimbri and Teutones were wild, ferocious fighters by the Celtic and Roman standards of the time: they showed no fear in battle and were prone to launching

Germanic warrior armed with throwing javelins. (*Photo and copyright by Ancient Thrace*)

Roman legionary wearing working dress, including a sun hat made of wicker. (*Photo and copyright by Aera Legio I Consularis*)

devastating frontal assaults. They fought as if they had nothing to lose, their only chance of ultimate survival being the possibility of finding new lands where they could settle. They came from an ancestral world that was completely different from that of the Celts and the Romans: they were used to surviving for many days with little food, and had no idea what a city was. For their entire life, the warriors of the Cimbri and the Teutones had lived in forests in cold temperatures, always having to fight for their survival. This made them harsh fighters who showed no respect for the military superiority of the Romans and who used battlefield tactics that had never before been encountered by the legions.

In 112 BC, the Roman Republic sent a large army to the Kingdom of Noricum, under the command of the consul Gnaeus Papirius Carbo. He was under orders to make an impressive show of force against the northern tribesmen in order to convince them that an invasion of Noricum was impossible. The Germani initially tried to negotiate with the Romans, asking for lands where they could settle, but it soon became clear that the legions had not crossed the Alps only to make a demonstration against them. As a result, the first battle between the Germani and the Romans was fought at Noreia, on the eastern borders of Noricum. This ended in disaster for the Roman legions and their Celtic allies, the Cimbri and Teutones crushing their opponents. Carbo escaped with his life only with great difficulty, and Rome's army that had been sent north was practically destroyed. The Romans had been taken by surprise, discovering that the Germani were completely different from any other people that they had encountered in battle. The determination and courage of the Germani were unrivalled in the Ancient World, even if their warriors had only very simple personal equipment that did not include a cuirass like those worn by the Romans and Celts. The legionaries were shocked by the fighting methods of these barbarians from the north, fear playing a significant part in the early defeats suffered by the Romans at the hands of the Germani. The Roman Senate punished Carbo for his defeat, removing him from his position as consul and causing his subsequent suicide. The Italian peninsula now lay open to invasion by the Cimbri and Teutones, the Alps having been crossed by the Germani and no other Roman troops remaining between them and the heart of Italy. When it seemed that a new sack of Rome was imminent, something quite unexpected happened: the Cimbri and Teutones, rather than moving south through Italy, instead turned west.

They crossed Switzerland and crushed the Helvetii confederation, one of whose tribes, the Tigurini, joined the Germani in their migration and moving with them towards Gaul. In 109 BC, the Cimbri and Teutones devastated most of Provence, after having defeated the local forces of Rome. This led to the creation of a stable and formal alliance between the Germani and the Celtic Tigurini, which was an extremely dangerous situation for the Romans. Within a few years, the Cimbri and Teutones had completely destroyed the network of alliances that Rome had created around the Alps for the protection of Italy: the Kingdom of Noricum had been invaded and sacked, part of the Helvetii had joined the newcomers and Roman Provence had been ravaged. The Senate sent a new army against the Germani in 107 BC, attacking a large camp that they had built at Burdigala (present-day Bordeaux). However, the Roman legions were ambushed by the Germani before they could reach the enemy positions and were massacred: some 10,000 Romans were killed in the clash and all the army's supplies were captured. After such a crushing defeat, most of the recently conquered Celtic communities of southern France rose up in revolt against Rome and joined the invaders. In 106 BC, the Romans sent another army to southern Gaul, which obtained some minor victories over the rebellious Celts. During the following year, however, a larger and much more decisive battle was fought between the legions and the Germani at Arausio. The Romans attacked a large encampment that had been built by the Cimbri with the intention of killing as many Germani as possible, but the assault was repulsed with heavy casualties and the Roman force was then massacred. After crushing the legions, the Cimbri assaulted and plundered the practically undefended Roman camp. The defeat at Arausio was particularly alarming for the Romans, the Germani having been able to crush a Roman army of over 80,000 soldiers. The Alpine passes were now again undefended, and the casualties suffered produced a serious lack of manpower for the Roman Army. Apart from the Battle of Cannae during the Second Punic War, Arausio was the worst defeat ever suffered by Rome. Indeed, apart from Hannibal, the Cimbri and Teutones were the most dangerous enemy ever faced by the Senate. However, the Germani did not attempt an invasion of Italy, strangely deciding instead to move further west and occupy Iberia. North-western Spain was at the time inhabited by several independent Celtiberian tribes, with the south-east half under Roman control. It is not know why the Germani again preferred not to invade Italy, although they were probably unaware that the Romans had no more troops and did not have much knowledge of the territories on which they were moving. It is important to note, however, that only the Cimbri invaded Iberia, whereas the Teutones preferred to remain in southern Gaul.

The Celtiberians were much more warlike than the other Celtic communities that the Cimbri had encountered during their migration: they were the result of an ethnic mix that took place between the Iberians and the Celts who settled in Spain and thus had some peculiar features that were not found among the Celtic inhabitants of Gaul. The Celtiberians had been at war with Rome for decades in order to preserve their independence and had been a fundamental component of Hannibal's Carthaginian

Roman *calo* (civilian servant attached to a legion) in working dress. (*Photo and copyright by Aera Legio I Consularis*)

Germanic warlord of the Cimbri and Teutones. (*Photo and copyright by Ancient Thrace*)

army. They were skilled horsemen and knew how to fight in the mountains of their homeland by using hit-and-run tactics. Such guerrilla methods had enabled them to defend their autonomy and defeat the Romans on several occasions. When the Cimbri invaded Iberia, the Celtiberian tribes formed a strong military alliance and moved against the Germani. We know very little of the war that was fought between the Cimbri and the Celtiberians, save that the latter were able to defeat the invaders (probably through an ambush) and forced them to go back to southern Gaul. The Cimbri were probably surprised by the combat capabilities of the Celtiberians, having previously been able to defeat several other Celtic communities quite easily. Meanwhile, the time spent by the Germani in Iberia was used by the Romans to reorganize their armies and the defences of Italy.

After the Battle of Arausio, the *terror cimbricus* ('fear of the Cimbri') was spreading in the Italian peninsula and the Senate feared that Rome would be destroyed by the wild Germani. Until the time of the Second Punic War, Roman armies were made up of citizen-soldiers who became conscripts only for a limited period of time (usually corresponding to the duration of a military campaign) and returned to their civil life as soon as their services were no longer needed. The citizen-soldiers had different personal equipment and tactical roles according to their *census*, i.e. their economic capabilities. During the Second Punic War, this military system revealed all its limitations, since the campaigns that were fought against Hannibal lasted for many years: being unable to return home after just a few months of military service, the citizen-soldiers could not work on their farms as they had always done, which caused great damage to the economy of the Roman Republic. Without the necessary manpower, Roman agriculture could not sustain a prolonged war effort. In addition, throughout the Second Punic War, the Romans had to send expeditionary corps to Iberia and Africa to fight against the Carthaginians who dominated those territories. This meant that thousands of Italic soldiers had to leave their homes for months or even years, being obliged to serve as professional soldiers rather than temporary recruits. During the great military emergency that followed the defeat at Cannae, Rome was obliged to recruit thousands of *proletarii* in order to replenish the losses suffered at the hands of the Carthaginians. The *proletarii* were the poorest citizens of Roman society, individuals who had never before been part of the military system because they were too poor to equip themselves properly (their only personal possession was the *prole*, i.e. their numerous sons and daughters). To face the menace of Hannibal, the Roman Republic gave the necessary personal equipment to thousands of poor citizens and admitted them into the ranks of the legions. Even when the Carthaginians were defeated, the Roman Army continued to recruit *proletarii* and gradually started to modify its organization.

After the Romans were defeated by the Germanic tribes of the Cimbri and Teutones at Arausio, it became apparent that a further great military reform had to be carried out, and the man to do this was Gaius Marius. One of Rome's greatest generals and a man of great experience, Marius had already fought at the head of an army on several occasions. He decided to transform the Roman Army into a force of professional soldiers coming from the poorest social groups of the Republic, who would serve in the army for most of their life and be equipped by the state. The era of the citizen-soldier was over: the new professional legionaries would earn a living from their military career and would be available to serve in every corner of the Mediterranean, with no limit on the duration of that service. Marius greatly improved the training and discipline of the Roman troops, giving to each legionary heavy personal equipment that included several working tools. Consequently, every soldier was able to operate as a combat engineer if needed, to build fortified encampments or destroy the fortifications of the enemy. Due to their new and much heavier equipment, the professional soldiers of the reformed Roman Army soon became known as the 'mules of Marius'. The reform that followed the disaster at Arausio also affected the tactics of the Roman Army, since Marius decided to abolish the differentiation in the weaponry carried by the legionaries. They were no longer divided into separate categories, but all received the same *panoplia* with chainmail and oval shield. Finally, the previous tactical organization with *manipuli* was replaced by a new one based on *cohorts*, which were stronger than the *manipuli* because they comprised a greater number of men and were thus well suited to face the massive frontal charges of the Celtic or Germanic warriors. Marius contravened the Roman constitution by being elected as consul for several years without interruption; in the eyes of the majority of the Romans, he was the only man who could save the Republic from destruction. The ambitious consul transformed the Roman Army into his own private force, creating strong personal links with his officers and introducing a new *esprit de corps* within the legions. He was the first, for example, to give a distinctive standard and a peculiar denomination to each unit of the Roman Army.

The main military unit of Marius' new Roman Army remained the legion: a large heavy infantry formation, entirely composed of volunteers having Roman citizenship. Each legion had approximately 5,500 men, divided into one elite *Cohors Prima* and nine 'line' cohorts. The First Cohort, formed by the best soldiers of the legion, had 800 men; the other nine cohorts each contained 480 legionaries. The *Cohors Prima* had five centuries of 160 men each, while the normal cohorts had six centuries with eighty legionaries in each. Each *centuria* comprised ten smaller units, formed of seven soldiers plus a single NCO known as a *decanus* and two non-

Germanic warrior of the Cimbri and Teutones. (*Photo and copyright by Ancient Thrace*)

The standard panoply of a centurion. (*Photo by Diego Casillas and copyright by Divulgación Histórica TANIT*)

combatants. This unit, known as a *contubernium*, was the smallest in the Roman Army. In addition, each legion had its own cavalry component: 120 horsemen divided into four *turmae*, with thirty soldiers apiece. Each *turma* was structured on three *decuriae*, the smallest cavalry units, each of which included eight soldiers, a *Decurio* (the equivalent of the infantry centurion) and an *Optio* (acting as an NCO). Most of the legionaries came from Italy, but as time progressed the provincial elements of the legions became increasingly numerous. The system of ranks of the Roman legion was a complex one, being specifically designed to make such a large body of soldiers work effectively. The overall commander of the legion was the *Legatus Legionis*, usually a senator with some solid military experience. The second officer in the chain of command was the *Tribunus Laticlavius*, who was generally a young member of the Senate with no military experience, who was assigned to the command of a legion in order to learn from the Legate. The third in command was the *Praefectus Castrorum*, who was responsible for the building and defence of the legion's camp; he was a long-serving veteran coming from the *equites* social middle-class, who had already finished his twenty years of service and had served as the most senior centurion in a legion. His functions included the training of soldiers and new recruits. The group of senior officers was completed by five lower-ranking tribunes known as *Tribuni Augusticlavii*, who all came from the equestrian class and already had a certain amount of military experience. They mainly performed administrative functions and commanded two cohorts each. The most senior centurion in a legion was called the *Primus Pilus*, who commanded the first century of the elite First Cohort. Once in battle, he had the honour to command the entire *Cohors Prima*. The other five centurions of the *Cohors Prima* were known as *Primi Ordines* and were considered to be superior in rank to their equivalents of the other cohorts. The centurions commanding the first centuries of the nine 'line' cohorts were called *Pili Priores* and were superior in rank to the *Primi Ordines* of the First Cohort. Like the *Primus Pilus*, each of these officers took command of his entire cohort in the event of a battle. Generally speaking, all centurions came from the lower social classes and became officers only thanks to their personal capabilities, making these experienced veterans the true backbone of the Roman Army. The commander of the four cavalry *turmae* was known as the *Tribunus Sexmentris*, and the decurion commanding each first *decuria* of horsemen had the honour to lead the entire *turma* in battle. The rank organization of the NCOs was particularly articulated, in order to perform a

Roman centurion with full combat equipment. (*Photo and copyright by Aera Legio I Consularis*)

Roman centurion wearing the characteristic helmet with transverse crest. (*Photo and copyright by Patrick Thierry*)

wide range of different functions. Each centurion directly appointed his adjutant and second in command, who was called an *Optio*. These performed more or less the same command functions as the centurion, but during battle had the important responsibility of remaining at the back of the century in order to keep the formation closed and to discourage deserters from abandoning the field. Each *Optio* had an adjutant known as a *Tesserarius*, who was third in the century's chain of command. The *Tesserarius* was the keeper of the watchword of his unit and performed several important administrative functions. The system of NCOs was completed by the ten *Decani*, each of whom commanded one of the *contubernia* that made up a century. Common legionaries could perform a series of special duties, which had a specific designation and corresponded to higher pay. The most important of these was the *Aquilifer*, the *Aquila* being the legion's standard and representing the valour of the whole unit; losing it was the greatest dishonour that a Roman legion could endure. As a result of this symbolic importance, its bearer was chosen from among the most experienced veteran soldiers. Each cohort had its own *Vexillum* (standard) that was carried by a special bearer known as the *Vexillifer*, while each century had its own *Signum* – a spear shaft decorated with medallions and topped with an open hand to signify loyalty towards the state – that was carried by a *Signifer*. Each century also had its own military music, consisting of a *Cornicen* or *Bucinator* and a *Tubicen*. These transmitted orders by playing their instruments and usually acted in close combination with the *Signifer*. The *Cornicen* played a horn, the *Bucinator* a particular kind of horn known as a *buccina* and the *Tubicen* a long trumpet.

In 102 BC, after the failure of their Iberian campaign, the Cimbri returned to southern Gaul and joined with the forces of the Teutones who had remained there. At this point they finally decided to move south towards Italy, it having become clear to them that they could not remain in Gaul. The local Celtic communities, after some initial enthusiasm for the newcomers, had changed their attitude and were now organizing themselves to expel the Germani. The powerful Arverni, in particular, had already attacked the Teutones and had no intention of accepting the presence of foreigners on the borders of their homeland. Marching through the region of Savoy, the Germani entered northern Italy with a two-pronged movement. The Teutones, in the west, invaded the Italian peninsula by marching along the coastal road that connected southern Gaul with Liguria; the Cimbri, in the east, crossed the Julian and Carnic Alps to attack Piedmont from the north. Gaius Marius, considering that the Teutones would reach the plains of northern Italy before the Cimbri – who had to cross the Alps – moved with all his forces against the former. He did not attack at first, but waited for the moves of the enemy. The Teutones tried to provoke the Romans in order to fight a pitched battle, but Marius continued to be prudent and grouped his forces into a large fortified camp. This was assaulted by the Germani, who were impatient to defeat the Romans, but their attack was easily repulsed by the Romans, the Teutones having no experience of conducting assaults against enemy fortifications. Unwilling to attempt another attack against the Roman positions, the Germani marched past Marius' camp and continued towards Italy. It took a total of six days for all the Teutones to move from their original positions, being slowed by their families and the wagons which they had with them. Marius did not attack the Germani while they were on the move, preferring to search for the perfect location where he could organize an ambush. During the following days, the Romans followed the enemy cautiously and closely, maintaining a distance from them and fighting several skirmishes with the rearguard of the Germani.

The Teutones eventually decided to stop and to face the Romans at Aquae Sextie, near modern Aix-en-Provence. The location of the battle had been chosen well by the Germani, since it consisted of a large plain on which they could deploy their superior number of warriors and launch a series of devastating frontal assaults. The Teutones, however, made a serious tactical mistake before the arrival of the Romans, failing to occupy some higher ground that dominated the battlefield and instead positioning themselves on a nearby plain. Marius, upon reaching the battlefield, rapidly occupied this high ground and gave precise orders to his legionaries: they were to wait for the frontal assault of the Teutones, then throw their javelins from the hill on the advancing Germani, draw their short swords and push the enemy back from the high ground. Marius thus intended to use the morphology of the terrain to his advantage: the Teutones would reach the Roman positions on top of the hill only after a long charge that would be conducted under a rain of enemy javelins and on broken terrain. Charging uphill in these conditions would be extremely difficult, even for excellent warriors like the Germani. As the battle commenced, everything went as planned by the Roman commander, the Teutones charging uphill but being decimated by the Roman javelins during their advance. The survivors who reached the top of the hill had to face a compact mass of legionaries, who were perfectly disciplined and ready to stop the *furor* ('fury') of the attackers. Despite showing great courage and determination, the Teutones were unable to dislodge the Romans from their strong positions and were pushed back downhill after suffering severe losses. Following several hours of combat, the battle had moved to the plain in the centre of the battlefield, where the Germani held their ground against the Romans. At this point, however, a chosen force of 3,000 legionaries was sent by Marius to attack the Germani from the rear. Now coming under strong pressure from two sides, the Teutones soon broke ranks and started to flee. This was the decisive moment of the battle, which was suddenly transformed into a massacre. The Romans relentlessly

Detail of a centurion's helmet. (*Photo and copyright by Aera Legio I Consularis*)

pursued the defeated Teutones, slaughtering many of the fleeing warriors. By the end of the battle, most of the Germani had been killed and all their families had been captured.

Following their defeat at the Battle of Aquae Sextie, the Teutones ceased to be a menace for Rome: more than 100,000 Germani had been killed or captured, including many women and children who were sold as slaves at the Roman markets. Teutobod, the leader of the Teutones, was able to escape from the battlefield with only some 3,000 warriors, but these were soon captured by the Celtic Sequani tribe. The Sequani were allies of the Roman Republic, so handed over the captured Germani to Marius. After obtaining such a brilliant victory, the Roman general mustered his surviving 37,000 men and marched against the Cimbri, who were advancing southwards. By July of 101 BC, the Germani were heading west along the banks of the River Po, the most important waterway in northern Italy that crossed the most fertile plains of the peninsula. The Romans deployed south of the Po in a strong defensive position, from where Marius initially tried to negotiate with the Germani instead of attacking

Detail of the *phalerae* (disc decorations) worn by centurions on their armour. (*Photo and copyright by Patrick Thierry*)

them. The Roman general tried to demoralize the Cimbri by parading in front of them the captured nobles of the Teutones. However, neither side had any intention of conducting serious negotiations: the Romans merely needed to gain time in order to reorganize their forces, while the Cimbri had to move south in order to survive. Marius selected a perfect location for the ensuing battle: an open plain known as the Raudine Plain (near present-day Vercelli). He now commanded an army of 52,000 soldiers, while the Cimbri could deploy some 120,000 warriors. After completing their preparations, the Romans moved north of the Po and offered battle to the enemy. Marius divided his forces into three groups: two wings, each with 16,000 legionaries, were made up of veteran soldiers who had already fought against the Teutones, while his centre comprised 20,000 soldiers who were new recruits with little military experience. The Romans deployed first on the battlefield and obliged the Cimbri to fight with the sun in their eyes. On the day of the battle, the Cimbri also had to deal with a keen wind that was blowing towards them. According to ancient sources, the Cimbri had a strong cavalry contingent with 15,000 horsemen deployed in front of their infantry, which consisted of more than 100,000 warriors assembled into an enormous square-shaped formation.

The Cimbri attacked first, the Romans having remained in their starting positions when the enemy appeared on the battlefield. While the Germani were advancing towards the Romans, Marius launched a rapid attack with his left wing against the right of the Cimbri. The Germani, however, responded to this move by arranging their forces into an enormous wedge formation that had the cavalry at the front. The Germani attacked with great violence and determination, pressing the centre of the Roman position, but despite their efforts they were not able to break the enemy lines and suffered very high casualties. At the same time, the cavalry of the Cimbri attacked the Roman right but were swiftly repulsed and routed by the superior mounted troops of Marius. The defeated Germani horsemen were pushed back towards the ranks of their infantry, causing great confusion among the Cimbri, who were unable to maintain order in their ranks. This was the key moment of the battle, the Roman right and centre advancing against the disordered Cimbri and killing many of their warriors. In terrible hand-to-hand fighting, the legionaries pushed against the Cimbri and pressed them into a confined space. This meant the Germani could not move properly and use their long slashing swords, while the Romans could easily employ their short stabbing swords to slaughter their opponents. Marius, with the left wing that was under his direct command, returned to the battlefield after having searched in vain for the Cimbri's right and attacked the Germani from the rear. The Cimbri were thus completely surrounded by the Romans and a massacre ensued. The Germani warriors also being weakened by the summer heat, they had

Centurion from the Early Imperial Period wearing scale armour. (*Photo and copyright by Legio XI C.P.F. Hispaniensis*)

Decorative torques (neck rings) worn by centurions. (*Photo and copyright by Aera Legio I Consularis*)

Roman centurion of the early Empire. (*Photo and copyright by Legio XIII Gemina*)

Centurion from the Early Imperial Period in marching order. (*Photo and copyright by Legio XI C.P.F. Hispaniensis*)

no option but to surrender or be struck down. Some surviving Cimbri retreated to the wagons that made up the rearguard of their army, where they attempted a last stand with the support of their women and children, but the Romans maintained their advance and slaughtered all the Germani, including their leader Boiorix. All the women and children who were not killed by the legionaries or who did not commit suicide were captured and later sold into slavery.

Having been resoundingly defeated, the Cimbri also ceased to be a menace to the territorial integrity of the Roman Republic, and the Cimbrian War thus came to an end. The war was a particularly important one from a historical perspective since it saw the first encounter between two vastly different civilizations: the northern Germani and the southern Romans. Rome had initially been taken by complete surprise by the fighting methods and determination of the northern warriors, but after the disaster at Arausio and the ascendancy of Gaius Marius, the Romans were able to recover. From a military point of view, the Cimbrian War was also a turning point in the history of the Roman Army, which transformed itself into a professional organization that was made up of volunteers serving as soldiers for most of their life. The new standard arms and armour and the new system of *cohortes* introduced by Marius remained unchanged for centuries, becoming fundamental components of Roman warfare. The Germani had learned a very harsh lessons during their attempted invasion of Roman territory. Having encountered the military power of the legions, they learned that a better organized army was able to defeat their warriors on the open field. Both the Cimbri and the Teutones were annihilated by the Romans, their entire population being either killed or captured. Their fate became well known among other northern barbarians, and during the following decades no other tribes attacked the borders of the Roman Republic.

# Chapter 8

# The Mithridatic Wars and the Conquest of Anatolia

The Kingdom of Pontus was founded in 281 BC by Mithridates I, who initiated a new Persian dynasty in the north-east of Anatolia by creating a new state. The region of Pontus, located south of the Black Sea on the northern coast of Anatolia, was part of Cappadocia under the Persian Empire and was later conquered by Alexander the Great. The Mithridatic royal house, which was to rule Pontus from 281 BC, belonged to the highest level of the Persian nobility: before the time of Alexander the Great, some members of this family had been the satraps (governors) of Phrygia. The arrival of the Macedonians did not greatly change their situation because they merely switched to recognizing Alexander as their new emperor and were thus able to retain their possessions. In 302 BC, however, Antigonus Monophtalmus (one of Alexander's successors) invaded Phrygia and killed the ruling Mithridatic satrap, whose son was able to escape from Phrygia with a handful of loyal retainers. After fleeing his country, he reached the north-eastern part of Anatolia, where he founded a new independent kingdom by bringing together the areas of northern Cappadocia and eastern Paphlagonia. The new king assumed the name of Mithridates I in 281 BC and proclaimed the royal dignity of his family. During the following decades, the various monarchs of Pontus fought against the other Anatolian states and the Galatians in order to expand their dominions. The forces of Pontus also launched a series of military campaigns against the Greek cities on the northern coast of Anatolia. The Mithridatic kings, with no access to the Mediterranean, had to find an alternative route for trade and commerce: the answer was the Black Sea, which soon became the centre of all Pontic economic and political activities. After conquering the Greek cities of the coast, Pontic expansionism invested the southern part of modern Ukraine (the region of Crimea) and the western coast of the Caucasus. Over time, the Pontic kings started to create very strong political and economic relations with the Greek cities (colonies) on the northern coast of the Black Sea and the Greek colonies on the Thracian coast (in the eastern part of modern Bulgaria). As a result of these moves, the Pontic rulers gradually became the masters of the Black Sea. Initially, Rome did not consider them a serious menace, having no interest of its own in the northern part of Anatolia. This situation changed in 116 BC with the ascendancy to the Pontic throne of Mithridates VI, who had great political ambitions. From 150 BC, the Kingdom of Pontus had been gradually 'hellenized' by the Mithridatic monarchs, who abandoned some of their Persian traditions as they modernized their country. The results of this process became clearly visible during the reign of Mithridates VI.

Unlike the previous kings of Pontus, including his father, Mithridates VI followed a strong anti-Roman agenda from the beginning of his reign. The main political ambition of the new monarch was to unite the whole Hellenistic world against Rome in order to restore the multinational empire of Alexander the Great. Differently from other Hellenistic monarchs, Mithridates perfectly understood the spirit of Alexander's political vision: he wanted to create a new multinational state in which peoples with different traditions and cultures could live and prosper in peace. The usual divisions between Macedonians/Greeks and Asian subjects had no sense for the new Pontic king, who was not of Macedonian descent. During the early phase of his reign, Mithridates conquered a large portion of Armenia (south of the Caucasus region) and the strategic Kingdom of Colchis (on the western coast of the Caucasus). The latter, in particular, was rich in natural resources: gold, wax, hemp and honey. In 101 BC, after having secured his empire in the Black Sea region, Mithridates started to expand in Anatolia and invaded the Kingdom of Cappadocia (which was given to his infant son). During the following years, the ambitious Pontic king also formed a strong alliance with the Kingdom of Armenia, which was now ruled by Tigranes II, who had married Mithridates' daughter, Cleopatra. These events made it clear to the Roman Republic that the expansionism of Pontus had to be stopped as soon as possible.

The First Mithridatic War broke out in 90 BC when the forces of Pontus invaded the Kingdom of Bithynia and then marched across the Roman province of Asia (the former Kingdom of Pergamon). The local Roman troops were unable to resist, leaving most of Anatolia in the hands of Mithridates. The Pontic invasion was supported by the Anatolians, who hated the Romans and their system of heavy taxation. In 88 BC, to present himself as the restorer of Hellenistic freedoms, Mithridates ordered the execution of 80,000 Romans and Italics living in the province of Asia. In the following months, most of the Greek cities joined Pontus in his war of liberation against the foreign invaders. Athens, in particular, had a prominent role in this process. In 87 BC, a massive Roman army under Sulla besieged Athens, and despite the military support of Pontus, Athens was eventually occupied by Sulla. During the following years, the Romans defeated Pontic armies in Greece on two occasions, Mithridates being forced to abandon Greece and come to terms with Rome. According to a peace treaty drawn up in 85 BC, Pontus had to relinquish all the territories that had been occupied in Anatolia: the Kingdom of Cappadocia, the Kingdom of Bithynia and the

Centurion from the Early Imperial Period in marching order. (*Photo and copyright by Legio XI C.P.F. Hispaniensis*)

Roman province of Asia. Nevertheless, the military capabilities of Mithridates in Asia remained intact. This led to the outbreak of the Second Mithridatic War from 83 to 81 BC, but it remained a local conflict that was fought on a small scale between the Roman forces based in Asia and part of Mithridates' army. At the end of the skirmishes that made up this conflict, nothing had changed from a territorial point of view.

In the following years, the ambitious Pontic monarch started to form new alliances against the Romans, allying himself with the pirates of Cilicia (who infested the Aegean Sea) and the Roman usurper Quintus Sertorius (who ruled the Roman territories in Spain, which had temporarily seceded from the central government of the Republic). In 75 BC, the last monarch of Bithynia died without heirs and left his kingdom to Rome, but two years later Mithridates invaded Bithynia, leading to the Third Mithridatic War. This time, military operations went in Rome's favour from the start, Pontic forces being compelled to retreat inside the borders of their homeland while Mithridates strove to avoid any direct military confrontation with the Roman legions. The Pontic king fled to Armenia, where he could count on the support of his ally Tigranes II. During the summer of 69 BC, the Romans invaded Armenia and defeated Tigranes II in a major pitched battle outside the Armenian capital of Tigranocerta. While the Romans were fighting against the

Roman veteran legionary of the late Republic. (*Photo and copyright by Aera Legio I Consularis*)

The *phalerae* (disc decorations) worn by centurions and veteran soldiers on their armour. (*Photo and copyright by Aera Legio I Consularis*)

remaining forces of Tigranes II in northern Armenia, Mithridates invaded Pontus in a bid to reconquer his kingdom. He was able to defeat the Romans in battle, causing a great change in the strategic situation of the war. The Roman forces now risked being isolated from their lines of supply, so they had to abandon Armenia without having decisively defeated Tigranes II. The following months were very difficult for Rome as Mithridates completed his reconquest of Pontus and the Armenians invaded Cappadocia. In 66 BC, however, Pontus and Armenia had to face a powerful army under the successful Roman general Pompey the Great (who had recently crushed the Cilician pirates in southern Anatolia). Pompey concluded a military alliance with the Parthians, who attacked Armenia and kept Tigranes II busy in the east; at the same time, Pompey marched with all his forces against Pontus. Mithridates was finally defeated in a pitched battle and was obliged to flee, the king marching with his few surviving forces to Colchis and then to Crimea. Meanwhile, in 65 BC, Pompey invaded Armenia and defeated Tigranes II. Mithridates was killed soon afterwards while reorganizing his forces for a defence of Crimea, his death apparently caused by a revolt of the army that was led by his son, Pharnaces. Following the death of Mithridates, the western half of Pontus was annexed by Rome, the eastern part being transformed into a small client kingdom that continued to exist until AD 62. The

Roman *Optio* of the manipular legion. (*Photo and copyright by Aera Legio I Consularis*)

Roman *Optio* with scale armour.
(*Photo and copyright by Patrick Thierry*)

Crimean possessions of Pontus, under the guidance of Pharnaces, became the new Bosporan Kingdom (a vassal state of Rome, which continued to exist for centuries).

During this period, Hellenistic Anatolia had three minor political entities that co-existed with the larger Kingdom of Pergamon: the Kingdom of Bithynia, the Kingdom of Cappadocia and Galatia. The Bithynians were one of the Thracian tribes that had migrated from Europe (modern Bulgaria) to Anatolia, as had the more numerous Phrygians. Despite being formally subjects of the Persian Empire, they had from 435 BC (well before the arrival of Alexander the Great) started to act as an independent realm. After 297 BC, the rulers of Bithynia started to call themselves kings, becoming fully autonomous in 281 BC. In 74 BC, the last monarch of Bithynia, having no heirs, bequeathed his kingdom to Rome, as had the last Attalid ruler of Pergamon. The independent Kingdom of Cappadocia was founded in 331 BC by Ariarathes, the last Persian governor of the Cappadocian satrapy. Since the Macedonians continued their advance towards the heart of the Persian Empire without attacking Cappadocia, Ariarathes was able to retain power in his province and avoided a direct confrontation with the army of Alexander the Great. Ariarathes was nevertheless defeated and killed by the Macedonians in 322 BC, but after a brief period of occupation Cappadocia again became independent in 301 BC under Ariarathes' son. The latter initiated a new royal family that was to last until 96 BC, when Mithridates VI of Pontus invaded Cappadocia and briefly annexed it to his possessions. With the defeat of Pontus, the Romans installed a new royal family in Cappadocia and transformed the small realm into a client kingdom. In 36 BC, the last exponent of the new dynasty died without heirs and thus the Romans gave Cappadocia to a local noble named Archelaus, who was a personal friend of Mark Antony. When Archelaus died in AD 17, Cappadocia was absorbed into the Roman Empire.

When the Celts invaded the southern Balkans in 280 BC, their hordes included a total of 152,000 foot warriors and 61,000 horsemen, a number of which crossed the Hellespont and entered Anatolia. The Celtic invaders apparently went to Asia at the invitation of Nicomedes I, King of Bithynia, who wanted their military help in a dynastic struggle against his brother. The Galatians who settled in the centre of Anatolia belonged to three different tribes: the Tectosages, the Trocmi and the Tolistobogii. These settled on the plateau of Phrygia after submitting the local inhabitants of Thracian descent, and this region, where the modern city of Ankara is located, soon started to be known as Galatia. The three tribes created a loose tribal federation, which exerted control over the subject Phrygian peasants. During the early phase of their settlement, the Galatians mostly supported themselves by plundering bordering countries or serving as mercenaries in the various Hellenistic armies of

Roman *Optio* with Attic helmet. (*Photo and copyright by Patrick Thierry*)

Roman *Optio* with scale armour. (*Photo and copyright by Aera Legio I Consularis*)

the time. In 232 BC, the Attalids of Pergamon finally defeated them in battle, which eventually led to the creation of a more permanent Galatian settlement in central Anatolia that became a vassal of Pergamon. In 189 BC, after defeating the Seleucids at Magnesia, the Romans launched a large expedition against the Celts of Anatolia and destroyed their state (for more details on the Galatian War, see Chapter 5). Thanks to the decisive help of the Romans, the Celts of Anatolia were later able to regain their independence after the end of the Mithridatic Wars. In 62 BC, Galatia formally became a client state of Rome and was officially organized as a kingdom, but it was finally annexed to the Roman Republic in 25 BC.

## Chapter 9

# The Conquest of Gaul

Gaul, the core of the Celtic civilization, was conquered by the Romans in a very short time compared to Iberia. Unlike what happened in Spain, the Celts living in present-day France had to face a single but incredibly effective Roman commander: Julius Caesar. Caesar started to rule Rome in partnership with Crassus and Pompey in 60 BC, when they formed the First Triumvirate. In 58 BC, after having been consul in Rome for one year, Caesar obtained the proconsulship of Cisalpine Gaul (northern Italy) and Transalpine Gaul (southern France). The great general and future sole ruler of the Republic badly needed a major military victory in order to consolidate his power and limit the ascendancy of his two colleagues/rivals. Crassus was the richest man of Rome and had already obtained a great military triumph to end the slave revolt of Spartacus, while Pompey had conducted and won many brilliant campaigns against some of Rome's fiercest enemies. Caesar was ambitious and had great personal capabilities, but unlike the other members of the Triumvirate he had never before been at the head of a large army. Obtaining command over the troops of the two Gauls was a great opportunity for him, as the pair of provinces were still border areas at the time, where a young and intelligent general could learn a lot from fighting against local tribes. The vast Celtic lands of central and northern Gaul were there for the picking for Caesar and his legions, who were already at their borders. Caesar knew that by conquering Gaul the Republic would become the greatest power of the time, as with the natural resources and population of Gaul at its disposal, Rome could have conquered all of continental Europe. Caesar had four veteran legions at his command and was ready to start his campaign of conquest: he only needed a *casus belli* to justify the outbreak of hostilities. This was provided for him by the Helvetii, who were coming under increasing pressure from the Germanic tribes living on their northern borders and were planning to migrate across Roman territory in search of a new homeland.

The Helvetii wanted to settle on the Atlantic coast of central Gaul, hoping to do so without having to fight during their journey. However, to reach their objective they had to cross Roman Provence and the territory of the Aedui (another Celtic tribe, the most important ally of the Romans among the Gauls). Caesar was extremely cunning in using this situation to his advantage, presenting the migration of the Helvetii as an invasion in order to force the Senate's hand and obtain permission to face this supposed menace with his legionaries. When the Helvetii started their journey, only one of Caesar's four legions was stationed in Transalpine Gaul. Being in no condition to mount an offensive, he initially tried to gain some time by holding peace talks with emissaries of the Helvetii. The tribesmen wanted to negotiate a safe and peaceful passage across Roman-held lands, having no intention of raiding or pillaging the areas they were to move across. After discussions lasting two weeks, during which he fortified his positions and raised more troops, Caesar rejected all the requests of the Celtic emissaries. At this point the Helvetii tried to enter Roman territory, but were easily repulsed by the new defences established by Caesar. Meanwhile, Caesar went to Cisalpine Gaul to raise two new legions and bring all his forces north of the Alps. Knowing full well that they were now going to face Caesar's full military might, the Helvetii initiated negotiations with the Sequani and Aedui to form a military alliance against Rome. The Sequani accepted and allowed the Helvetii to cross their lands without opposition, but the Aedui remained loyal to Rome and saw their territory devastated by the migrating Helvetii. Responding to an Aedui request for help, Caesar attacked the Helvetii with three legions while they were crossing the River Arar. When the Romans arrived, three of the four Helvetian tribes had already crossed the river and Caesar was able to destroy the remaining one. Caesar, however, continued his pursuit with great determination. During the ensuing Battle of Bibracte, fought in 58 BC, the Roman legions were finally able to crush the Helvetii, who suffered enormous losses. The few survivors surrendered to Caesar and were sent back to their homeland, where they lived in peace as subjects of Rome.

Victory over the Helvetii, however, did not end the hostilities in Gaul, the Sequani and Aedui continuing to fight against each other after their territories were freed of the Helvetii. The two tribes, probably the most powerful ones in Gaul at the time, were fierce rivals and had been at war for a long time. The main reason that the Aedui had become loyal allies of Rome was that they needed a powerful ally to prevail in their frequent wars with the Sequani. Around 64 BC, shortly before the arrival of Caesar, Gaul was already in turmoil as the three strongest Celtic nations on its territory fought against each other. The Arverni and Sequani had established a strong military alliance and started to attack the Aedui. The Aedui had been Rome's most important allies in Gaul for decades, and could thus count on military support from the Republic. The territory of the Aedui was located between those inhabited by the Arverni and the Sequani. If the Aedui were defeated, their homeland would be partitioned between their rivals. The Arverni and Sequani wanted to control the main waterways of France in order to obtain supremacy over Gaul's most important commercial routes. The Germanic warlord Ariovistus and his Suebi tribesmen, living

Roman *Optio* wearing *phalerae* and torques. (*Photo and copyright by "Aera Legio I Consularis"*)

Legionary from the Early Imperial Period with *lorica hamata* armour and phalerae decorative disks. (*Photo and copyright by Legio XI C.P.F. Hispaniensis*)

on the eastern bank of the Rhine, took advantage of the conflict that ravaged a large portion of present-day France and intervened by forming an alliance with the Arverni and Sequani. Ariovistus had been an ally of Rome, receiving from the Senate the honorific title of *Rex Germanorum* ('King of the Germani'). Indeed, the Germanic leader exerted control over all the Germanic communities that had settled on the borders of Gaul along the Rhine. Ariovistus, however, was pursuing the interests of his tribe and not those of Rome.

In 63 BC, the Suebi crossed the Rhine in great numbers and joined forces with their Celtic allies, which soon after led to the decisive Battle of Magetobriga in north-eastern Gaul. We know very little of this clash, the greatest battle ever fought between two Celtic armies. According to ancient sources, Ariovistus was at the head of 15,000 Suebi warriors. These played a prominent role during the clash and showed their military superiority, turning the tide of battle in favour of their allies. The clash at Magetobriga was extremely important to the history of Gaul, the defeated Aedui being forced to become vassals of the Sequani, while the Suebi were permitted to settle on the western bank of the Rhine. This situation was impossible for Rome to accept, having supported the Aedui during the conflict but with insufficient resources. The arrival of the Germani in Gaul revolutionized the political situation in the region and the balance of power that the Romans had gradually enforced there. Indeed, Magetobriga can be seen as the real *casus belli* that provoked the Roman military intervention in Gaul. Soon after being defeated, the Aedui sent ambassadors to Rome asking for help against their enemies. Meanwhile, Ariovistus was given one-third of the land previously inhabited by the Sequani in exchange for his intervention and was permitted to settle 120,000 Suebi in Gaul close to the Rhine. Once the Germanic presence in Gaul had become quite significant, Ariovistus turned against his former allies and attacked the Sequani. His warriors raided and terrorized the Celtic settlements of north-eastern Gaul, in search of lands where immigrants from the eastern bank of the Rhine could settle. Ariovistus' demands for another third of the Sequani's lands were deemed unacceptable and caused a strong reaction among many of the Celtic communities. Soon after the Battle of Magetobriga, it became clear that the Germani had entered Gaul only to assume dominance over the region and not to simply act as allies of the Arverni and Sequani. Initially, Rome tried to establish a positive relationship with Ariovistus, but the Republic was actually just preparing for war against the Germani in view of their future expansionist moves. When Caesar arrived in Gaul in 58 BC, he sent ambassadors to summon Ariovistus to a conference, but the leader of the Germani refused to meet him. The Roman general responded to this affront by once again sending his ambassadors to Ariovistus' camp, this time with a precise

Roman *Aquilifer*. (*Photo and copyright by Aera Legio I Consularis*)

series of requests: the Germani were formally forbidden to transfer more families to the western back of the Rhine, were required to return all the hostages they had obtained from the Aedui after Magetobriga and were forbidden from waging war on any Celtic tribe (especially on the Aedui). Ariovistus was offended by Caesar's requests, the Germanic warlord wanting to assert his right to exact tributes and take hostages from the defeated Aedui.

The Suebi rapidly prepared for war and established their main base at Vesontio, a location that had been particularly important commercially for the Aedui. Caesar advanced with his legions towards Vesontio and, before attacking the Germani, tried to come to terms with Ariovistus. The Romans' position in Gaul was not yet very strong and the ambitious general probably wanted to avoid a direct confrontation with the warlike Suebi. After a lengthy meeting, which came to nothing, Caesar and Ariovistus returned back to their respective camps and prepared their troops for battle. The Germanic leader realized that Caesar had come to Gaul only to submit the Celtic tribes and not to bring peace, as claimed by Roman propaganda. The Romans built a fortified camp in front of Vesontio and at first did not attack. Ariovistus responded to this move by harassing the enemy almost every day but refusing to accept battle on the open field. The leader of the Suebi organized a special task force made up of cavalry and light infantry, who were tasked with conducting skirmishes against the Romans. The Romans had great difficulties in dealing effectively with the hit-and-run tactics of the Germani, the support of the light infantry making the Germanic cavalry stronger than the Roman mounted corps. Ariovistus' skirmishers were extremely effective and were eventually able to cut Caesar's line of supplies. The Roman forces were running the risk of becoming isolated in hostile territory. Being in a very difficult position, almost surrounded by a superior enemy army, Caesar was left with no choice but to attack the Germani and try to obtain a decisive victory. The ensuing clash – known as the Battle of the Vosges or Battle of Vesontio – was a particularly violent one. As was their traditional practice, the Germani deployed their families and wagons at the rear of their battle formation and prepared to defend their camp. Caesar attacked with six legions and a large number of auxiliaries. The Romans first attacked the left wing of the Germanic host, but before the legionaries could throw their javelins against the enemy line, the Suebi launched a furious frontal attack. The Germani advanced with such speed that the Romans could not fully deploy their forces, and for a moment it seemed that the Suebi were gaining the upper hand. The legionaries were pushed back by the Germani and suffered severe casualties during hand-to-hand fighting. But in the decisive moment of the battle, Caesar launched his reserves to attack the right wing of the enemy. The Germani had used all their resources in the centre of the battlefield and had no reserves of their own: as a result, the Roman attack broke their lines and won the day for Caesar. The Suebi, together with their families, fell back to the Rhine, but many were slaughtered by the Roman cavalry that followed in close pursuit. Ariovistus and some surviving Suebi were able to cross the river by using some small boats or by swimming, but most of the Germani were killed or captured (including Ariovistus' family). After the Battle of the Vosges, the Suebi ceased to be a threat to Gaul and Caesar was free to conquer most of present-day France during the following years.

In 57 BC, another quarrel between Celtic tribes gave Caesar the opportunity to start a new campaign. This time the threat to Rome's Gallic allies was represented by the Belgae, a powerful confederation of Celtic tribes living in the northern part of Gaul (present-day Belgium). The Belgae were extremely strong militarily and had experienced very little contact with the Mediterranean world, instead being heavily influenced by the Germanic tribes living on the other side of the Rhine. The Belgae confederation had been formed during 58 BC in order to counter Caesar's increasing political influence over Gaul, but this was interpreted as a threat by the Aedui and the other local allies of Rome, who feared that such a powerful grouping could conquer most of Gaul. Caesar's operations against the Belgae proved to be extremely difficult, with the Romans almost defeated at the Battle of the Sabis River (57 BC). This clash, however, proved to be decisive for the destiny of the Belgae, as Caesar was afterwards able to destroy most of their settlements and gradually crush the resistance of the Belgian Celts, who had lost most of their best warriors at the Sabis River. By the end of the year, all the lands of the Belgae were in Roman hands, after which it became clear even to Caesar's Gallic allies, such as the Aedui, that Rome was gradually conquering the whole of Gaul by using the internal divisions of the Celts.

In 56 BC, Caesar moved against the Celts of Armorica, who had formed a tribal confederation, following the example of the Belgae, in the hope that this could stop Roman expansionism. The lands of the Armorican Celts included Brittany and Normandy and were strongly linked to the Celtic communities living in Britain. The Armorican confederation also included the important tribe of the Veneti, the only Celtic community to have seafaring capabilities and a fleet of warships. The campaign against the Veneti proved a very difficult one for Caesar, who had to build a fleet on the English Channel and fight with all his resources, both on land and at sea. Thanks to an intelligent use of innovative amphibious tactics, however, the Romans were finally able to prevail over the Armorican Celts and defeated them on the difficult terrain of Normandy. Caesar also mounted two punitive expeditions on the borders of Gaul in 55 BC, one against the Germani and the other against the Britons. After the defeat of Ariovistus and his Suebi, other Germanic tribes living on the eastern side of the Rhine had continued to mount frequent raids against

Roman *Signifer*. (*Photo and copyright by Aera Legio I Consularis*)

Gaul. In order to show his Celtic allies that he was still the protector of Gaul, Caesar organized a punitive campaign against the Germani, crossing the Rhine to punish the raiders on their homeland. The Germani and the Celts were greatly impressed by Caesar's subsequent actions, the Romans building a massive bridge over the Rhine and crossing the river with a large army. No other military leader – Roman or Celtic – had ever achieved anything similar, so the Germanic tribes were taken by surprise and defeated quite easily. After this victory, Caesar turned against the Britons in order to punish them for the support given to the Celts of Armorica during the previous year. The Romans disembarked in southern England with two legions, but this time Caesar's campaign was only a partial success, bad weather destroying a large part of the Roman fleet and the landings being opposed very effectively by the Britons (who employed war chariots on a large scale, which the Romans were not prepared to face). Caesar returned to Britain in 54 BC at the head of a larger military force, this time having made comprehensive preparations to face the Britons on equal terms. The Catuvellauni, the most important Celtic tribe in southern England, were defeated and obliged to pay a yearly tribute to Rome. Caesar's expeditions in Britain had not gained any new territories for Rome, but were extremely important propaganda for the general: no previous Roman commander had ever ventured so far north, reaching the edge of the known world.

Julius Caesar was at the peak of his power, but the tribes of Gaul were now on the verge of revolt. Having seen the fall of the Helvetii, Belgae and Armoricans, it was by now clear that Caesar wanted to rule the whole of Gaul and the only way to stop him was to form a national confederation of Celts to fight against the Romans. Some Gallic leaders began to realize that unity was a key factor: the Celtic tribes had been defeated by Caesar because they had fought without coordination and because some important groups, like the Aedui, had preferred to help the Romans for their own political advantage. A true sense of Gallic identity gradually developed, especially following the most recent campaigns of Caesar. In 54 BC, the Eburones of northern Gaul revolted against the Romans. Having previously been vassals of the Belgae, they were now under the guidance of their charismatic leader Ambiorix and mounted a full-scale rebellion against Rome. Caesar had a total of 9,000 men garrisoning the territory of the Eburones, but these were mostly inexperienced levies without previous combat experience. Consequently, when the revolt of Ambiorix began, they were easily defeated by the Eburones and expelled from their lands. The Eburones then tried to raise a general revolt of all the Belgae, but the arrival of Caesar with a large number of troops prevented them from achieving their objective. In 53 BC, after several months of harsh fight, 50,000 well-trained Romans were finally able to crush the Eburones and their allies (including some Germanic tribes). Northern

Gaul was thus brought back under Roman control, but only after severe difficulty. Meanwhile, in the centre of Gaul, the most powerful Celtic tribes were assembling their forces under the leadership of Vercingetorix, who would become the greatest Gallic warlord of all.

Vercingetorix had become king of the Arverni by popular support after defeating the faction of his tribe that wanted to maintain peace with the Romans. Thanks to his charismatic leadership, he was able to unite all the tribes of central Gaul against Rome, founding a new Gallic capital at Gergovia (near modern Clermont-Ferrand) and obtaining support from all social groups around Gaul. Before his rise to power, only the aristocrats of the various tribes had been determined to fight against the Romans, the common peasants and farmers having never been particularly enthusiastic to risk their lives against Caesar's legionaries. Vercingetorix proposed a new vision to the whole Celtic world, one which comprised a much more democratic approach to political issues, which gave him the complete support of the lower social classes and enabled him to raise massive armies. Vercingetorix became supreme commander of

Roman *Vexillifer* bearing the insigna that signalled the presence of a member of the Senate with the legion. (*Photo and copyright by Aera Legio I Consularis*)

Veteran legionary from the Early Imperial Period drinking from his canteen made of wicker. (*Photo and copyright by Legio XIIII Gemina*)

all the region's Celtic troops in 53 BC, when for the first time in Gallic history he imposed strict military discipline and secured for himself the loyalty of all the tribes by taking aristocratic hostages. Instead of fighting against Caesar in a pitched battle, he preferred defending certain key locations of his territories by exploiting to the full the natural fortifications provided by the terrain. The great Gallic warlord undertook a scorched earth strategy, burning villages and fields to prevent the Romans from living off the land. This caused some discontent among the Celts but also enormous logistic difficulties for Caesar, who soon ran out of supplies and was obliged to provoke the enemy to fight a decisive battle as soon as possible. This clash took place at Gergovia, Vercingetorix's capital, where the Celts prevailed and for the first time defeated the Romans in a major battle. However, the Gauls suffered many casualties and were unable to mount an effective pursuit of Caesar's retreating legions. Indeed, both sides needed time to reorganize their forces; Vercingetorix, in particular, was waiting for the arrival of massive reinforcements from other areas of Gaul. Consequently, he decided to retreat to the most important stronghold in Gaul: Alesia, a fortified city that was considered unconquerable by most contemporary observers. After replenishing his troops, Caesar marched to besiege Alesia, building a first wall around the city in order to isolate the defenders from the rest of the world. However, a massive force of 100,000 Celtic warriors arrived at Alesia to reinforce Vercingetorix, and Caesar risked being trapped between two large Gallic armies, one surrounding his legions and the other behind the walls of Alesia. To deal with this crisis, Caesar ordered the construction of a second wall to protect his legions from assault by the Celtic reinforcements. Joint attacks by the Gauls, mounted from inside as well as outside, came close to defeating the Romans, whose defences were almost broken. Only a desperate counter-attack launched by Caesar with his last reserves saved the legions from total defeat. After the failure of these assaults, however, the Gallic reinforcements were routed and abandoned Vercingetorix to his fate. He finally surrendered when he ran out of supplies, after an incredible but ultimately hopeless resistance. With Alesia captured, Gaul had finally fallen to Caesar, bringing to an end centuries of Celtic prosperity.

Caesar's armies that conquered most of Gaul in just a few years did not only comprise Roman legionaries, substantial support being provided by a series of auxiliary contingents of non-Roman professional soldiers. These included mercenaries or allies who were extremely loyal to Caesar and performed specific tactical functions. It is important to remember that after the military reforms carried out by Gaius Marius during the Cimbrian War, the Roman legions had adopted a new structure that did not comprise light infantry but only *cohortes* of heavy infantry. Thereafter, the Romans had to rely on foreign soldiers in order to deploy sizeable contingents of light troops. It was a similar situation with the cavalry, which had never been a fundamental component of the Roman Army. During his Gallic campaigns, Caesar deployed the following auxiliary contingents: Celtic heavy cavalry, Germanic light cavalry, mounted skirmishers recruited from the Numidians and the Mauri, Cretan archers, Balearic slingers and Iberian light infantry. The Celtic heavy cavalry came from the tribes of Gaul that were allied with Rome, most notably the Aedui, and were equipped with helmet and chainmail, spears and long slashing swords. Mounted on tall horses, these cavalry made up a shock force that was employed by Caesar on several occasions and with great success. The Germanic light cavalry, instead, were equipped as light skirmishers: they did not carry armour or helmets

Roman *Cornicen* of the manipular legion. (*Photo and copyright by Aera Legio I Consularis*)

and were armed with throwing javelins. These horsemen were of great use for conducting reconnaissance missions as well as to harass the enemy with rapid incursions. On some occasions they were also employed to launch frontal charges, and were always considered by Caesar to be a fundamental component of his forces. In 55 BC, the Roman troops operating in Gaul included a total of 400 Germani, who were all nobles from the tribes that had been defeated by Caesar and then served alongside the Romans (together with their servants) as hostages. Their presence on Rome's side was a sign of good will and trust, which had great political importance. Caesar was particularly impressed by the martial spirit of the Germani, admiring them for their courage and their simple way of life (which was seen as ideal to forge good warriors). The 400 Germanic cavalry who served as part of Caesar's army were supported by a number of light infantry, the servants of the Germanic nobles, trained to run alongside the horsemen in order to cover their flanks during close combat. Caesar encountered this peculiar tactical formation invented by the Germani during the campaign against Ariovistus, and soon realized that it had a great potential. As a result, he was the first to create combined units of infantry and cavalry inside the Roman Army. These later became known as *cohortes equitate* and remained an important component of the Roman military machine for

Roman *Cornicen*. (*Photo and copyright by Aera Legio I Consularis*)

many years. The light infantrymen of the Germani who ran alongside the cavalry clung to the manes of their horses, and were mostly tasked with stabbing at enemy mounts. With the outbreak of Vercingetorix's rebellion, many allied Celtic horsemen abandoned Caesar, who was obliged to recruit more Germani from the eastern bank of the Rhine to replace them. These numbered some 600 men, as usual accompanied by their servants/light infantrymen. The Germanic warriors of Caesar fought with enormous valour on several occasions against Vercingetorix and always routed any Celtic cavalry whom they faced. The Germani who participated in the final Gallic campaign of 52 BC also followed Caesar during the ensuing years, taking part in all the conflicts that were fought by their general, most notably the civil war that ended with the defeat of Pompey at the Battle of Pharsalus. In 45 BC, Caesar returned to Rome and finally disbanded the auxiliary corps of his army. The surviving Germanic veterans went back to their homeland after having travelled far and wide around the Mediterranean and plundered many different countries.

The Numidians and Mauri serving with Caesar were equipped as mounted skirmishers and used javelins as their main weapons. As they had done as part of Hannibal's Carthaginian army, they performed as scouts and were masters at organizing ambushes. Caesar's Cretan archers and Balearic slingers were all mercenaries, who were well known in the Mediterranean world for their incredible fighting skills. Crete and the Balearic Islands were home to two of the most important light infantry 'schools' of Antiquity, where the deadliest archers and slingers were trained as professional soldiers from childhood. The Iberian light infantrymen were known as *caetrati*, because they carried a small round shield called a *caetra*. They were armed with deadly short swords and with javelins, and Caesar appreciated them for their great tactical flexibility. The Roman forces in Gaul fighting under Caesar apparently also included a small number of Iberian cavalrymen, who carried heavy personal equipment.

Roman *Cornicen* wearing chainmail. (*Photo and copyright by Aera Legio I Consularis*)

Roman *Cornicen*. (*Photo and copyright by Aera Legio I Consularis*)

## Chapter 10

# The Parthian War of Crassus and Herod's Judaea

The fiercest enemy of the Roman Republic in the Middle East was the Parthian Empire, a major military power of Asia that had combat capabilities comparable to those of the Romans. The Parthians, originally a nomadic people living in north-eastern Iran, had gradually carved out an empire in the Middle East under the guidance of their ambitious Arsacid dynasty. Taking advantage of the Seleucid Empire's great internal and external difficulties, they had conquered the whole of Iran and later reached the borders of Syria (the heartland of the Seleucids) after having established themselves in Iraq. Parthian armies consisted entirely of cavalry, with mounted archers armed with deadly composite bows and heavy cavalrymen covered with armour. The Seleucids were defeated on several occasions by this combination of light and heavy cavalry, which was extremely effective tactically. The Parthians could fight for long periods in desert areas and had an excellent logistical organization, while their archers were superb skirmishers who could fire their arrows with great accuracy, even when their horse was running away from their target (this being the famous 'Parthian shot'). The Parthian heavy cavalry, or cataphracts, were equipped with long spears and rode armoured horses. When charging at full gallop, they often proved unstoppable. When the Seleucid Empire crumbled, the Romans occupied Syria and its other western regions in 64 BC, while the Parthians took over Iraq and other areas in the east. It subsequently became apparent that the two emerging powers of the Middle East would soon clash for dominance of the whole region: the Romans wanted Iraq, while the Parthians wanted Syria. The first major Roman–Parthian War took place from 54–53 BC when Crassus, one of the members of the First Triumvirate together with Pompey and Caesar, attempted to earn some military glory by invading Parthia. The campaign saw the participation of Crassus' son, Publius Crassus, who was a young but already experienced cavalry commander who had served in Gaul under Caesar and brought with him a large contingent of Celtic auxiliary cavalry. The Romans assembled a force of seven legions for the invasion of Parthian territory, supported by 4,000 light infantry and 4,000 cavalry (including the 1,000 Celtic heavy horsemen commanded by Crassus' son). Instead of attacking the Parthians from Armenia, the Romans decided to take the direct route through Mesopotamia in a bid to capture the region's major cities. The Parthian king,

Legionary from the Early Imperial Period with the 'subarmalis' padded armour that was worn under the metal cuirass. (*Photo and copyright by Legio XI C.P.F. Hispaniensis*)

Orodes II, responded by assembling an army of 9,000 mounted archers and 1,000 cataphracts, which was sent to harass the advancing invaders under the command of the experienced general Surena. The legionaries marched into the most desolate part of the Mesopotamian desert without having any knowledge of the terrain and being far from any source of clean water.

The Romans encountered Surena's Parthians at Carrhae. Surprised by the presence of the enemy, Crassus deployed his troops into a hollow square, each side comprising twelve cohorts. Initially, the Parthians did not attack, allowing the Romans to reach a nearby stream, where they could have camped for the night. However, Crassus and his son decided to launch an immediate attack without allowing their soldiers a rest. Surena then surrounded the Roman square with his horse archers, who engaged the legionaries from a distance. The powerful composite bows of the Parthians were capable of piercing the Roman shields, and Crassus' heavy infantry soon started to suffer heavy casualties. The legionaries repeatedly advanced towards the Parthians in an attempt to engage them at close quarters, but the horse archers simply retreated and let loose their famous 'Parthian shots' as they withdrew. At this point the Romans deployed themselves in their testudo

Levantine auxiliary archer of the early Empire. (*Photo and copyright by Legio XIII Gemina*)

defensive formation for more protection against the enemy arrows, but they were then charged by the enemy cataphracts. The heavy Parthian cavalry did not break the Roman square, but caused some losses to Crassus' legionaries with their long spears. The Romans hoped that they could hold out until the Parthians ran out of arrows, but Surena had thousands of camels transporting missiles to resupply his mounted archers. Realizing he was in a desperate situation, Crassus sent his son against the enemy mounted archers at the head of a task force that comprised 1,000 Celtic heavy cavalry, 500 archers and eight cohorts of legionaries. The Parthian horse archers merely feigned retreat and drew off the attacking Romans. When the task force was sufficiently separated from the rest of the Roman troops, they came under attack from the Parthian cataphracts while the mounted archers cut off their line of retreat. Outnumbered and surrounded, the Celtic cavalrymen and Roman legionaries resisted to the last man, Publius Crassus committing suicide in order to avoid capture. Crassus, unaware of his son's fate, ordered a general advance of his troops, only to discover the head of Publius Crassus on a Parthian spear. At this point of the battle, the Parthian horse archers surrounded the legionaries and shot at them from all directions, while the cataphracts launched several frontal charges that broke the cohesion of the Romans. The onslaught continued until nightfall, when the surviving Roman soldiers retreated to the nearby settlement of Carrhae. Four Roman cohorts became lost in the dark and were wiped out by the Parthians. On the second day of the battle, Surena proposed a truce to the Romans and a meeting took place between him and Crassus, but during the talks the Roman leader and his officers were massacred by the Parthians. The Parthians were said to have poured molten gold down Crassus' throat, in a symbolic gesture mocking the Roman general's renowned greed. Following the death of their leader, the surviving Romans were all captured or killed after attempting to flee from Carrhae. Roman losses amounted to some 20,000 killed and 10,000 captured, making Carrhae one of the costliest military defeats in Roman history. The Roman prisoners were deported to eastern Iran, where they married local women. Surena, meanwhile, was executed by Orodes II, the king being jealous of his general's glorious victory. After the battle, the Parthians tried to invade Syria, but were repulsed by the local Roman forces after some indecisive fighting, hostilities then coming to an end.

After the death of Alexander the Great and the end of the Successor Wars between his squabbling generals, Judaea had become part of the Seleucid Empire. Initially, the Jews accepted Seleucid dominance with no particular problems, their new rulers permitting them to practice their religion in peace. This situation changed dramatically in 168 BC when Antiochus IV launched a major programme of forced 'hellenization' that was unacceptable to the Jews. When the Seleucid monarch ordered an end to the ancestral law of the Jewish people and forbade circumcision, Judaea rose up in revolt under the charismatic leadership of Judah the Maccabee. The ensuing conflict between the Maccabees and the Seleucids was extremely violent, with victories and defeats on both sides. Initially, Judah the Maccabee was able to defeat the Seleucids in a series of small engagements by making an intelligent use of guerrilla warfare, thanks to which he was able to enter Jerusalem in 164 BC. In 161 BC, however, the Jewish rebels were defeated in a pitched battle by the Seleucids. Judaea's new-found freedom seemed under threat, but the Jews were able to resist and maintained their independence. Guided by the brother of Judah the Maccabee, Jonathan the Hasmonaean, they were able to initiate a new dynasty of kings. Taking advantage of the civil wars that ravaged the Seleucid Empire during those years, the first Hasmonaean monarch was finally able to obtain effective independence for Judaea. Formally, however, the Jews remained subjects of the Seleucids until the reign of John Hyrcanus I (135–107 BC), one of the greatest Hasmonaean kings, who obtained formal independence from the Seleucids and even expanded his kingdom by conquering new territories (such as Idumaea in the south, which was inhabited by warlike Arab nomads). Within a few decades, Judaea became an important regional power, with great political ambitions. In 66 BC, however, civil war broke out after the death of King Alexander Janneus and his wife Salome Alexandra, the throne of Judaea being contended by the two sons of the former king (who acclaimed themselves Hyrcanus II and Aristobulos II). Hyrcanus was supported by one of his father's most important courtiers, Antipater the Idumaean, but the internecine conflict continued. In 63 BC, both brothers asked for a military intervention by the Romans, who had a large army in nearby Syria under the command of Pompey the Great. Deciding to intervene in favour of Hyrcanus, Pompey swiftly defeated the supporters of Aristobulos. The Roman help, however, came at a high price: in 57 BC, Judaea was divided into five small and self-governing territories that were all client states of Rome.

In 40 BC, Judaea was invaded by the Parthians, who had temporarily overcome the Roman forces in Syria. The invaders wanted to reunite the country under a puppet king, Antigonus II (son of Aristobulos II, the pretender defeated by Pompey). The only man willing to lead a fight against the superior forces of the Parthians and their client king was Herod (later known as Herod the Great), son of Antipater the Idumaean. Against all odds, Herod was able to defeat Antigonus II after three years of warfare and reconquered the whole of Judaea thanks to Roman help. Under Herod the Great, the Jewish army became an excellent military force and conducted several victorious campaigns of territorial expansion, most notably against the Nabataeans. Herod had become Rome's most important ally in the Middle East, and was even

Gallic auxiliary heavy cavalryman. (*Photo and copyright by Marilyn Paléri of the historical reconstruction association Lorica Romana*)

able to fight on equal terms against the Ptolemaic forces of Cleopatra. When the great king died in 4 BC, however, the destiny of Judaea changed forever: the country was divided between the three sons of the former king, forming three self-governing territories that were again Roman client states. The most important of these was annexed by Rome in AD 6, being followed by the other two during the following decades.

Roman legionary cavalryman of the early Empire. (*Photo and copyright by David Burns of Legio XIIII Gemina*)

Roman legionary cavalryman of the early Empire with parade helmet having facial mask. (*Photo and copyright by Legio XIII Gemina*)

Legionary cavalryman from the Early Imperial Period. (*Photo and copyright by Legio XI C.P.F. Hispaniensis*)

# Chapter 11

# Roman Weapons and Tactics

With the manipular reform of the Roman Army, each of the four categories of soldiers that made up the Republic's infantry received a distinctive panoply. The *velites* were equipped with helmet, round shield, light javelins and short sword; the *hastati* with helmet, rectangular breastplate (*pectorale*), oval shield, one heavy javelin, one light javelin and short sword; the *principes* with helmet, chainmail (*lorica hamata*), oval shield, one heavy javelin, one light javelin and short sword; and the *triarii* with helmet, chainmail, bronze greaves, oval shield, long spear and short sword. Following the reforms of Gaius Marius, the arms and armour of the *principes* were adopted by all the legionaries, with just one modification since the light javelin came out of use. During the whole period taken into account in this book, the Roman cavalry was equipped with the following panoply: helmet, chainmail or muscle cuirass, round shield, short spear and short sword.

The standard Roman *galea*, or helmet, used by the *velites*, *hastati* and *principes* was the Montefortino type. This was very easy to produce, the Romans copying it from the Celts, introducing some minor adjustments that were needed to transform the Montefortino into the standard helmet of the legions. The name of this model of *galea* derives from the location in Italian where the first helmet of this kind was discovered. The Montefortino had a round shape with a raised central knob and protruding neck guard; the former was usually surmounted by coloured plumes, while the latter was generally decorated with incisions. It also had a pair of cheek pieces, which could be of two main kinds, according to their shape. The first model of cheek pieces reproduced the stylized shape of the cheek, whereas the second one was trilobate, consisting of three small discs in the shape of a triangle. Apparently, trilobate cheek pieces were influenced by the helmets and armour of the Italic peoples, which frequently included this peculiar combination of three discs. Over time, this type of cheek piece was abandoned and the other one became dominant, being adopted by the Romans. Montefortino helmets had many positive features: they were easy to produce, gave excellent protection to the wearer's face, could be easily decorated in many different ways and were comfortable enough to be worn for a long time. All these characteristics made the Montefortino the most popular helmet of the Roman Republican period. During the closing decades of the Republic, however,

Back view of an auxiliary cavalryman from the Early Imperial Period. (*Photo and copyright by David Burns of Legio XIIII Gemina*)

another helmet designed by the Celts and later adopted by the Romans co-existed with the Montefortino: the Coolus helmet. This new type had a simple round shape, with a ridge running around its base; on the back, this ridge enlarged to become a neck guard, similar to the one of the Montefortino. In addition, the Coolus helmet had a couple of cheek pieces that reproduced in a stylized way the human cheek. Extremely easy and cheap to produce, the Coolus helmet became extremely popular, especially with the auxiliaries of the Roman Army. Archaeological finds suggest that cheek pieces were only added to Coolus helmets at a later date, as a result of the Montefortino's influence. Consequently, at least initially, the Coolus helmet had the appearance of a simple metal cap. Crest fittings were only added at a later time. The *triarii*, instead of the Montefortino, wore the old-fashioned Italo–Corinthian helmet, which had three thin slits in the plate protecting the face, two for the eyes and a vertical one for the mouth and nose. On the back, a large curved projection protected the nape of the neck. When not fighting, a soldier could wear his Italo–Corinthian helmet tipped upward for comfort: most of his face would thus have been freed by the frontal plate, that would have assumed an oblique position. The cavalry of the Roman Army were mostly equipped with the Boeotian helmet, which was perfect for such use, being completely open on the face, allowing good peripheral vision and permitting unimpaired hearing. It consisted of a domed skull surrounded by a wide and flaring down-sloping brim, which came down at the rear to protect the back of the neck but also projected forward over the forehead to work as a sort of visor. The sides of the brim had a complex shape, comprising downward-pointing folds that protected the lateral areas of the face. Basically, the Boeotian helmet was a bronze version of the Greek Petasos sun hat, which was widely employed by the Thessalian cavalry. In particular, it had the same shape as the Boeotian version of the Petasos hat (which was worn by the Boeotian cavalry and was characterized by the presence of the downward-pointing folds on the sides).

The Roman *lorica hamata* was an improved version of the Celtic chainmail, which was designed for the first time during the fifth century BC. It consisted of thousands of small iron rings linked together in order to form a mesh, the rings interlocked in a way that created something similar to a knitted sweater. Depending on its dimensions, a chainmail was made up of some 30,000 metal rings and weighed approximately 10kg. Roman chainmail usually covered the legs to the knees and was generally sleeveless, but had reinforcement panels for the shoulders that were attached across the top of the back and held at the front by a bar-and-stud device. A double thong was stretched from the rings attached just above the inner corners of cut-outs to the outer corner of each of the reinforcement panels. The edges of these panels were bound with rawhide in order to create a raised border. The panels could have angled

Legionary cavalryman from the Early Imperial Period wearing scale armour and parade helmet with facial mask. (*Photo and copyright by Robert Vermaat/Ala I Batavorum*)

The standard panoply of a Roman legionary cavalryman of the early Empire. (*Photo and copyright by Legio XIII Gemina*)

or rounded off ends on the chest, and could be made of iron rings like the rest of the armour or be of leather. The Roman *lorica hamata* comprised alternating rows of closed washer-like rings punched from iron sheets and rows of riveted rings made from drawn wire that ran horizontally, producing very flexible, reliable and strong armour. Each ring had an inside diameter of about 5mm and an outside diameter of 7mm. Up to 30,000 rings went into a single *lorica hamata*, each of which took about two months to produce, even with continual slave labour at the state-run factories. Although this kind of armour was labour-intensive to manufacture, it could, with good maintenance, be used by a soldier for several decades. Officers and cavalrymen of the Roman Army widely used the 'muscle cuirass', a type of body armour cast to fit the wearer's torso and designed to mimic an idealized human body. It was cast in two pieces, the front and the back, which were later hammered together. The cuirasses of officers were highly ornamented with sculpted mythological scenes or other rich decorations. The muscle cuirass tended to be used in combination with fringed strips of leather known as pteruges at the armholes and at the lower edge of the cuirass.

Most of the Roman legionaries used oval shields, which were copied from Celtic ones. The oblong Roman oval shield, or *scutum*, originally had a central spine made of wood and a boss (*umbo*) of metal, which was designed to reinforce the whole

Roman legionary cavalryman of the early Empire wearing helmet of the Weiler model. (*Photo and copyright by Legio XI C.P.F. Hispaniensis*)

Roman legionary cavalryman of the early Empire with chainmail. (*Photo and copyright by "Legio XI C.P.F. Hispaniensis"*)

structure of the shield. Bosses were oblong and could have different shapes. The main body of the shield was made of oak planks, which were chamfered to a thinner section towards the rim, while the wooden spine, swelling in the middle, was shaped in order to correspond with a round or oval cut-out in the shield's centre. The strap-type metal boss crossed over the wider section of the spine and was riveted on the external surface of the shield. The outer surface, on both sides or only on the front, was entirely covered with leather and could be painted in various bright colours and have decorations of several kinds. Bosses corresponded to the handle of the shield on the back and thus had a fundamental function in protecting the user's hand. Additional

Roman legionary cavalryman of the early Empire with parade helmet having facial mask. (*Photo and copyright by Robert Vermaat/Ala I Batavorum*)

Legionary cavalryman from the Early Imperial Period equipped for parade. (*Photo and copyright by Robert Vermaat/Ala I Batavorum*)

Roman legionary cavalryman of the early Empire with scale armour. (*Photo and copyright by Robert Vermaat/Ala I Batavorum*)

Detail of a Montefortino helmet. (*Photo and copyright by Aera Legio I Consularis*)

metal binding was frequently attached to the external edges of the shield in order to reinforce it. The shields carried by the light infantry and cavalry were generally smaller than those of the heavy infantry and had a more circular shape. Most of the Roman shields were painted red and were decorated with highly standardized devices such as eagles' wings, Jupiter's lightning bolts, stylized wild beasts and laurel wreaths.

The first weapon to be used in battle by a Roman legionary was the *pilum*, a heavy javelin specifically designed to kill enemies from a distance or to limit them in the use of their shields. The *pilum* was extremely difficult to remove after hitting a shield or cuirass. It had a barbed head and a long narrow socket or shank, made of iron mounted on a wooden haft. The barbs were designed to lodge in the enemy shields so that the whole javelin could not be removed. The long iron shank prevented the head from being cut from the shaft. A *pilum* weighed between 1kg and 2kg, which gave the weapon great power of penetration. The shank, due to its peculiar function, was made of softer iron than the hard pyramidal tip; after hitting an enemy shield, the intention was for the shank to bend in order to render both weapon and shield useless. The shank of the *pilum* was joined to the wooden shaft by either a socket or a flat tang, which was designed to break when the javelin hit its objective. Consequently, when a clash was over, the Roman soldiers could retrieve the wooden shafts from the battlefield and reuse them with a new tip and shank. The *pilum*, in most cases, had a spike on the other end of the shaft that made it easier to dig into the ground. Sometimes, the javelin could also be weighted by a lead ball in order to increase its power of penetration. The maximum range of a *pilum* was approximately 35 metres, although the effective range was some 15–20 metres. The *velites* were not equipped with the *pilum*, instead receiving a lighter javelin known as a *verutum*. This had a shaft that was about 1.1 metres long, much shorter than that of the *pilum*. The tapering point of the *verutum* measured about 13cm and had inferior armour-piercing capabilities compared with that of the heavier *pilum*. The *verutum* had a very simple design, lacking both the shank and tang of the *pilum*. Both the cavalry and the *triarii* were equipped with a thrusting spear known as a *hasta*. This had an elongated iron point – with the edges curving inwards from the belly of the blade to its tip – and a wooden shaft. The average length of the *hasta* was 2 metres, including a butt spike made of iron, although for the *triarii* it could be longer.

The *gladius* short sword, the most iconic and important weapon of the Roman Army, was actually not Roman at all. The true origins of this weapon are much clearer if we use its complete and proper name, the one used by the Romans: *gladius Hispaniensis*. The *gladius* was first designed in Iberia (modern Spain and Portugal), as confirmed by various Roman sources but also by archaeological evidence. It was created by the Celtiberians, one of the many warrior peoples inhabiting Iberia during the Iron Age. Differently from the other Iberian communities, the Celtiberians were of mixed descent, being the product of Celtic migrations across the Iberian peninsula. Because of their Celtic heritage, the Celtiberians constructed weapons with innovative techniques. The Romans abandoned their traditional Greek-style swords after the Second Punic War as a result of their many battlefield encounters

Detail of a Coolus helmet. (*Photo and copyright by Patrick Thierry*)

Coolus helmet. (*Photo and copyright by Aera Legio I Consularis*)

with the Celtiberian allies/mercenaries of Hannibal. They decided to adopt the same short swords as their Celtiberian opponents after recognizing that the *gladius* had great tactical potential. According to the latest metallurgical studies conducted on surviving Roman short swords, the *gladius* could be forged following two different kinds of manufacture: it could be produced from a single piece of steel or as a composite blade. Swords produced with the first process were created from a single bloom by forging from a temperature of 1,237°C. The carbon content increased from 0.05–0.08 per cent on the back of the sword to 0.35–0.40 per cent on the blade, from which we can deduce that some form of carburization may have been used. Swords produced

Detail of a Roman straw hat. (*Photo and copyright by Patrick Thierry*)

with the second process were crafted by the pattern welding process from five blooms reduced at a temperature of 1,163°C. Five strips of varying carbon content were created: the central core of the sword contained the highest concentration of carbon (0.15–0.25 per cent); on its edges were placed four strips of low-carbon steel (with a concentration of 0.05–0.07 per cent), the whole thing welded together by forging on the pattern of hammer blows. Each blow increased the temperature sufficiently to create a friction weld at that spot. The forging operation, the most important of the whole process, continued until the steel was cold, producing some central annealing. When produced by welding different strips together, the *gladius* had a channel down the centre of the blade; when made by fashioning a single piece of steel, the blade had a rhomboidal cross-section. The blade of the *gladius* was two-edged for cutting and had a tapered point for stabbing during thrusting. A solid grip on the weapon was provided by a knobbed wooden hilt added on the blade, usually having ridges for the fingers. The hilt, known as a *capulus*, could be decorated in many ways, the swords of high-ranking officers, for example, usually having a hilt sculpted to resemble the head of an eagle. Sometimes the blade could be ornate too, for example with the owner's name engraved or punched on it. The original Iberian sword, used from around 200–20 BC, had a slight 'wasp-waist' or 'leaf-blade' curvature which made it quite different from the following models. It was the largest and heaviest model of *gladius* ever produced, with a blade length of 60–68cm and an overall length of 75–85cm. The blade was 5cm wide, with the overall weight of the weapon being 900g. The *gladius* was carried in a scabbard mounted on a belt or, more frequently, a shoulder strap. It was worn on the left side of the soldier's body, so a legionary had to reach across his body to draw it. Centurions, to differentiate themselves from their soldiers, wore the *gladius* on their right side.

During the late Republican period, Roman cavalry replaced their short Greek-fashion swords with the longer *spatha* or cavalry sword. This, originally designed by the Celts, had a distinctive elongated leaf shape. It was double-edged and had a square-kink or shallow 'V' point (the sides of which were drawn at an angle of 45 degrees to the axis of the blade). The tang of the *spatha* – the internal part of the handle, made of metal but covered with organic material – swelled sharply to a point of greatest width that was just below its centre. The *ricasso* – the unsharpened length of blade just above the handle of the sword – was very short and had a notch that could vary greatly in depth. Sword handles were made of wood or leather and generally had the form of an 'X', continuing the pattern of the famous Celtic 'antennae' swords. The handle was completed by a pommel, which was connected to the tang by a rivet-hole. The blade measured from 60–90cm in length and was made of iron or steel. Generally, blades had a broad neck, with the greatest width usually low down towards

Standard Roman *gladius* of the early Empire. (*Photo and copyright by Legio XIIII Gemina*)

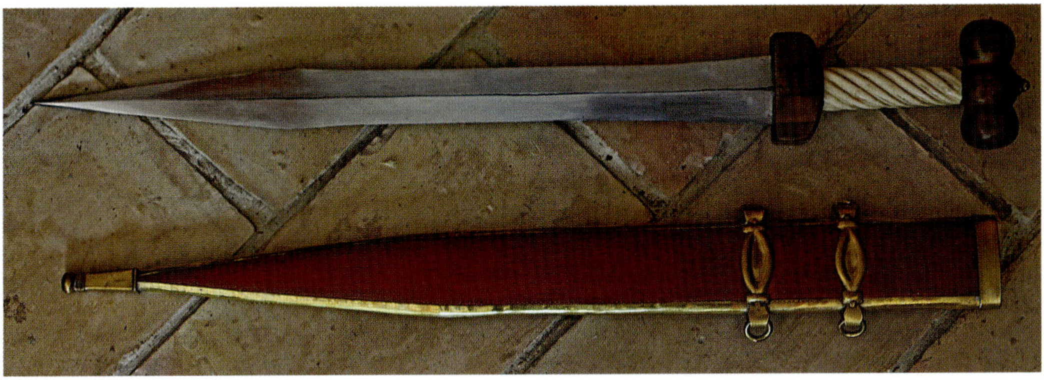

Early example of *gladius Hispaniensis*. (*Photo and copyright by Aera Legio I Consularis*)

Example of a decorated *gladius* from the Caesarian period. (*Photo and copyright by Aera Legio I Consularis*)

the point. Over time, points became increasingly rounded, which confirms that these cavalry weapons were used for slashing and not for thrusting. Roman long swords were transported in iron scabbards, richly decorated with incisions and/or bosses. Scabbards reproduced the general shape of the blade and were constructed from two plates: the front one, slightly wider than the back one, was folded over the latter along the sides. Each scabbard was reinforced by a decorated band around the top and a sculpted chip at the bottom. Scabbards were generally suspended on the right hip from a leather belt, and the sword was suspended from the waistbelt by means of a metal loop located on the back face of the scabbard. During the late Republican period, each Roman legionary also started to carry a short dagger known as a *pugio*. This was intended as an auxiliary stabbing weapon, specifically designed for hand-to-hand combat. Like the *gladius* short sword, it was designed by the Celtiberians and later adopted by the Romans. The *pugio* had quite a large leaf-shaped blade, which usually narrowed from the shoulders to run parallel to about halfway along its length before narrowing to a sharp point. A midrib ran close to the length of each side, either standing out from the face or sunken by grooves. The tang was wide and flat, while the grip was riveted through it, as well as through the shoulders of the blade. The pommel was originally round, but it soon assumed a new trapezoidal shape. Each *pugio* was transported in its own sheath made of soft metal, which had four suspension rings and a bulbous terminal expansion that was pierced by a large rivet. The hilt consisted of two layers of horn or wood. Each *pugio* was 18–28cm long and 5cm wide. The sheath could be heavily decorated, especially for the daggers used by officers.

From the days of Gaius Marius' military reforms, the Roman heavy infantrymen became famous for their capabilities as combat engineers, building fortified camps or military infrastructure such as bridges in all conditions and on every kind of terrain. As a result, each legionary carried a *sarcina*, or military pack, which comprised several important pieces of equipment. The *sarcina* consisted of a *furca*, or carrying pole, to which the following objects were suspended: a *loculus* (leather satchel), waterskin, small bag with rations of food for fifteen days, shallow *patera* dish, cooking pot, skewer, some pointed stakes (*sudis*) used to construct fortifications, a *dolabra* pickaxe, *ligo* mattock, a *falx* to clear overgrowth, *batillum* shovel and basket for hauling earth. The equipment of each legionary was completed by the '*cingulum militare*, or military belt, which had a very important symbolic significance: wearing it meant being part of the army, since civilians used different types of belt. Depriving a soldier of his military belt meant expelling him from the army. The *cingulum militare* was a leather belt decorated with iron fittings and consisting of the following components: the *baltea* (hanging band), the *bulla* (rivets that were applied on the *baltea*), the *pensilium* (pendants that were applied at the end of the belt's straps), the *lamna* (a disc that was applied at the end of each apron strip embracing the *pensilium*) and the *fibula* (the buckle of the belt).

The main garment worn by the Roman soldier was the tunic, which was usually short-sleeved but was also produced in a version with long sleeves, known as the *tunica manicata*, which was common in the northern territories of the Republic. The Roman tunic, made of wool for winter and of linen for summer, was a simple T-shaped garment reaching the knees of its wearer. It was not made of cut-and-sewn

*Pugio* of a legionary from the early Empire. (*Photo and copyright by Legio XIIII Gemina*)

A nice example of *pugio*. (*Photo and copyright by Aera Legio I Consularis*)

parts, but was woven entire in a single piece, each *tunica* being folded in half and sewn up the sides, with a neck slit cut in the centre. The standard colours for military tunics were red and white, the latter being particularly popular in the hotter regions of the eastern provinces. After the tunic, the cloak was the second most important garment for the Roman soldier. Made of wool and containing natural oil in order to repel water, it could be of two different kinds, known as *sagum* and *paenula*. The *sagum*, typical of the Italian peninsula, was rectangular in shape, whereas the *paenula* was rounded and had a hood (*cuculia*) for protection of the head. All cloaks reached the hips and were double-folded so that they did not fall beneath the knees when worn. The cloaks of officers were different from those of soldiers, since they were longer (ankle-length) and trapezoidal in shape. All cloaks were pinned up on the right shoulder by a large brooch (*fibula*), which could be richly decorated if worn by a senior officer. The trousers, known as *bracae*, were considered by most well-educated Roman citizens to be a 'barbarian' garment, but the legions garrisoning the northern frontiers adopted them on a large scale from the late Republican period. All legionaries wore a *focale*, or scarf, around their neck, made of wool for cold months and linen for hot months. The *focale* protected the neck from chafing by the armour and was loosely knotted at the front. Regarding footwear, all Roman soldiers wore the open sandals that later became known as *caligae*. These were made from leather and were laced up the centre of the foot and to the top of the ankle. Iron hobnails were hammered into their sole for added strength.

Rank distinctions existed in the Roman Army. A centurion, for example, was distinguished as follows: he carried the *gladius* on the left side and the *pugio* on the right (the legionaries did the opposite); he had a peculiar transverse crest on the helmet; he always carried a vine-stick (*vitis*) that was used to mete out punishments; and he applied sculpted gold, silver or bronze discs known as *phalerae* on the front of his armour. The *phalerae* were military medals, usually awarded for distinguished conduct in action. They were aligned in three horizontal lines and were attached to orthogonal leather straps to form a single breastplate that was worn on the chest. An *Optio* was easy to recognize since he had plumes of horse hair or feathers applied on either side of his helmet (with the standard crest in the middle), although he also carried a long wooden staff (*hastile*) that was as tall as the *Optio* himself and had a round metal pommel at its end. Like the vine-stick of centurions, this was used to hand out punishments. All standard-bearers carried a peculiar small round shield and wore a fur over their shoulders and head: a wolf one for the *Vexillifer* and a lion or tiger for the *Aquilifer*. The fur was worn as a cape, with the head of the animal strapped to the helmet of the standard-bearer. In many cases, the standard-bearers, being veterans,

Roman knives used as working tools. (*Photo and copyright by Aera Legio I Consularis*)

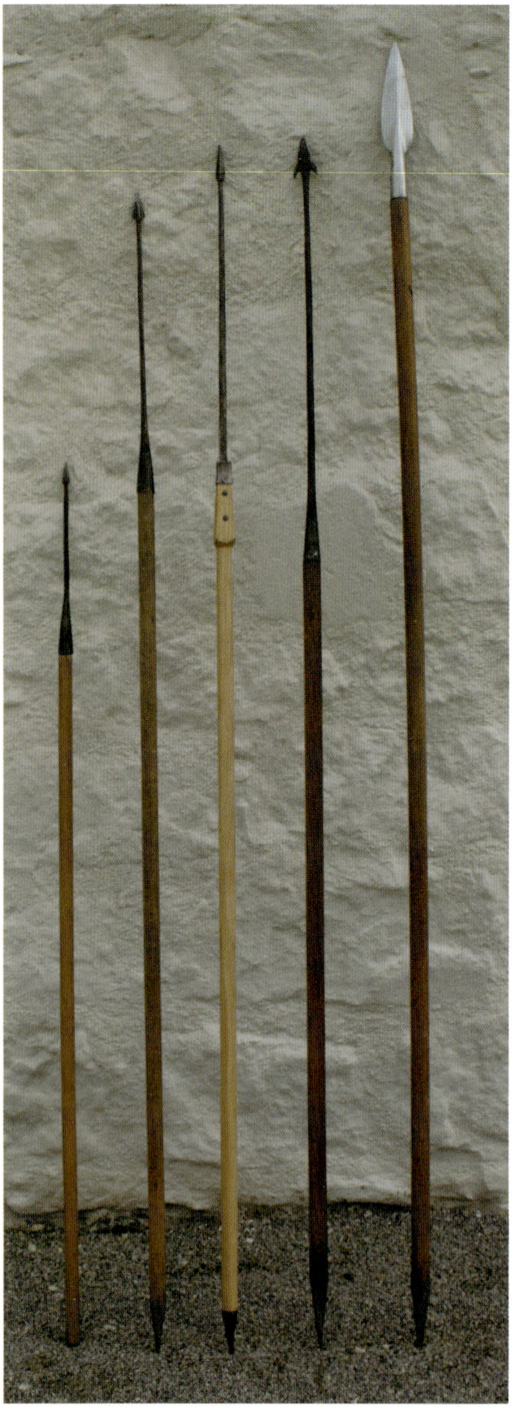

Different types of Roman javelins (*pila*) and a spear (first on the right). (*Photo and copyright by Legio XIII Gemina*)

wore on the chest the same *phalerae* as the centurions. The military musicians of a legion were usually equipped like the standard-bearers, carrying small round shields and wearing a fur over their shoulders and head.

Roman battle tactics were highly standardized but incredibly effective. The first weapon to be used in a pitched clash, as we have seen, was the *pilum*. Later, once the enemy ranks had been shattered by the initial rain of javelins, the legionaries drew their short swords and charged their opponents. According to the Roman tactical doctrine, emphasis was put on using the *scutum* shield to provide maximum body coverage, while the *gladius* was used to attack with devastating thrusts and short cuts. Adopting such basic tactics, the Romans were usually able to defeat any enemy infantry formations for many centuries. This kind of warfare also limited the number of casualties suffered by Roman troops. Using their swords to thrust in the few spaces created between the shields of their close formations, the legionaries were rarely exposed to the offensive weapons of the enemies, who had very limited opportunities to manoeuvre. Like the *gladius*, the *pugio* dagger was a short stabbing weapon. It was used as a secondary arm during the most intense hand-to-hand fighting, especially when space for movement became very limited or when the *gladius* could not be used for whatever reason. Intensive and continuous training made

Two examples of Roman oval *scutum*; the one on the right has the protective cover made of leather that was used on campaign. (*Photo and copyright by Aera Legio I Consularis*)

Roman military belt, decorated with bronze fittings. (*Photo and copyright by Aera Legio I Consularis*)

The personal objects carried by each legionary in his leather bag. (*Photo and copyright by Aera Legio I Consularis*)

The inside of a centurion's tent. (*Photo and copyright by Aera Legio I Consularis*)

the Roman legionaries efficient killing machines. The stabbing wounds produced by their short swords were almost always mortal, especially if hitting the abdominal area (intended as the main target for thrusts from the early phase of a legionary's intensive training). Each Roman infantryman was trained to adapt to any possible combat situation: each of his weapons could be used in different ways and he had to be ready to exploit to the full any mistake made by the enemy or any favourable momentum. For example, Roman legionaries were trained to slash kneecaps beneath their shield wall or to cut the throat of their enemies while charging in close formation. Such tactics enabled Roman armies to dominate the battlefield throughout Europe and the Mediterranean world for much of the Republican period.

# Bibliography

**Primary sources**

Appian, *Roman History*
Appianus, *Gallic History*
Appianus, *Illyrian Wars*
Appianus, *Wars in Spain*
Cassius Dio, *Roman History*
Diodorus Siculus, *History*
Diodorus Siculus, *Library of History*
Dionysius of Halicarnassus, *Roman Antiquities*
Livy, *History of Rome from its foundation*
Plutarch, *Lives*
Polybius, *The Histories*
Strabo, *Geography*

**Secondary sources**

Allen, S., *Celtic Warrior 300 BC – AD 100* (Osprey Publishing, 2001).
Anderson, E.B., *Cataphracts: Knights of the Ancient Eastern Empires* (Pen & Sword, 2016).
Bishop, M.C. & Coulston, J.C., *Roman Military Equipment From the Punic Wars to the Fall of Rome* (Oxbow Books, 2006).
Brzezinski, R. & Mielczarek, M., *The Sarmatians 600 BC–AD 450* (Osprey Publishing, 2002).
Connolly, P., *Greece and Rome at War* (Frontline Books, 1981).
Cowan, R. & O'Brogain, S., *Roman Guardsman 62 BC–AD 324* (Osprey Publishing, 2014).
D'Amato, R., *Roman Centurions 753–31 BC* (Osprey Publishing, 2011).
Gorelik, K., *Warriors of Eurasia* (Montvert Publishing, 1995).
Kiley, K.F., *An illustrated Encyclopedia of the Uniforms of the Roman World* (Lorenz Books, 2012).
Matthews, K.D., *The Early Romans: Farmers to Empire Builders* (McGraw-Hill Books, 1973).
Newark, T., *Ancient Armies* (Concord Publications, 2000).
Newark, T., *Ancient Celts* (Concord Publications, 1997).
Newark, T., *Barbarians* (Concord Publications, 1998).
Newark, T., *Warlord Armies* (Concord Publications, 2004).
Nicolle, D. & McBride, A., *Rome's Enemies 5: the Desert Frontier* (Osprey Publishing, 1991).
Quesada Sanz, F., *Armas de Grecia y Roma* (La Esfera, 2014).
Rocca, S., *The Army of Herod the Great* (Osprey Publishing, 2009).
Rostaing, N., 'Lost Pontic legions: Pontic imitation legions used by Mithridates', *Ancient Warfare Magazine*, volume X, issue 3.
Sumner, G., *Roman Military Clothing (1): 100 BC–AD 200* (Osprey Publishing, 2002).

Travis, J. & Travis, H., *Roman Body Armour* (Amberley, 2012).
Travis, J. & Travis, H., *Roman Helmets* (Amberley, 2015).
Travis, J. & Travis, H., *Roman Shields* (Amberley, 2014).
Warry, J., *Warfare in the Classical World* (Salamander Books, 1997).
Webber, C., *The Thracians 700 BC–AD 46* (Osprey Publishing, 2001).
Wilcox, P., *Rome's Enemies 1: Germanics and Dacians* (Osprey Publishing, 1982).
Wilcox, P., *Rome's Enemies 2: Gallic and British Celts* (Osprey Publishing, 1985).

# The Re-enactors who Contributed to this Book

## Aera Legio I Consularis

We are a non-profit re-enactment association with volunteer members animated by a common passion for ancient Roman history. We strive to be as authentic as possible in order to understand how things were and try our best to show to the public an accurate view of the Romans of the time period we represent. We have chosen the period extending from the Second Punic War to Julius Caesar for several reasons. First, because it is the period of Rome's largest expansion: when it started, Rome more or less controlled the Italian peninsula, and at its end, it controlled 85 per cent of the Mediterranean basin. This period, strangely lesser-known than others of the Roman era, was a turning point in Rome's history that led to a change of regime. It also saw the creation of a Roman province in southern France that later became today's Provence, from where our founding members originate. Our researches led us very early on to work with historians and archaeologists, as well as with other specialists from various countries. We are pursuing a dual objective, like Janus on our logo: research on the one hand and public information on the other. Our aim is to be as accurate as possible in what we show to the public, so we work hard to make exact reproductions instead of using generic, commercially available models. Each reproduction has its particular use, and by manipulating it we better understand its original use. We can then share this with the public. Dressing, manipulating and training with replicas teaches us many things and helps us better understand our ancestors. We are proud to work with museums and historical monuments around our continent, in order to give some life and understanding to all these otherwise static beauties. Thanks to our reproductions, the public, and also museum curators, can interact with us and manipulate objects that otherwise they could never have touched. Their reaction and enthusiasm are what give us the strength to continue our work. We have historians and archaeologists inside the group, but we exchange many experiences with external archaeologists and various specialists from different countries. The construction of an exact replica requires some degree of expertise and, over the years, we have built up the knowledge necessary to find a better solution to obtain the best reproduction possible. Our members come not only from different nations but also from different social backgrounds. The first things that we have in common are passion and dedication. We are open to all kinds of people. Sharing a cultural passion and looking in the same direction is our mission, just like in the time of the ancient Romans.

*Contacts:*
E-mail: centurion@reconstitution-romaine.com
Website: www.reconstitution-romaine.com
Facebook: https://www.facebook.com/legionIconsularis/

Some objects used by the legionaries to prepare their food. (*Photo and copyright by Aera Legio I Consularis*)

## Ala I Batavorum

Some clouds of dust on the horizon, slowly heading in your direction… It turns out to be a squad of Roman cavalrymen, fully armed, with shiny armour and highly decorated horses. The approaching horsemen wear a silver mask, blinking in the sun, their faces covered, only showing their eyes: spectacular, yet also terrifying. Stichting Ala I Batavorum recreates these cavalrymen from ages gone by. In our regular shows, our fully equipped cavalrymen show their skills at arms on horseback. Equipment and tactics are shown and explained, both in single file as well as operating in a group. Thus, all equipment and the tactical advantage of the cavalry within the

Roman Army are explained to the public. It is highly entertaining: a spectacular and educational show that will have people talking about it for some time. Stichting Ala I Batavorum can bring together up to six cavalrymen. All our equipment is based upon archaeological records and is well researched. Our impressions focus mainly on the Batavian auxilia cavalry, but also include Augustean and late Roman versions. Most impressive is our late Roman *clibinarius* kit, incorporating a recreation of Dura Europos (Syria) horse scale armour.

*Contacts:*
E-mail: info@ala-batavorum.nl
Website: www.ala-batavorum.nl
Facebook: https://m.facebook.com/ALA-BATAVORUM-133726753365976/

A centurion inspecting his legionaries. (*Photo and copyright by Aera Legio I Consularis*)

## Divulgación Histórica TANIT

Divulgación Histórica TANIT is a small non-profit group hailing from Mérida in Spain, formed by a group of people passionate about ancient history and the Phoenician–Punic culture. Our aim is to communicate about history using public engagement and historical re-enactment (both civilian and military), as well as the manufacture and acquisition of replicas of elements of the Phoenician–Punic, Roman and pre-Roman cultures of the Iberian peninsula. We do this by always using written and iconographic sources, together with the advice of historians and archaeologists. Our focus on the military side is the period of the Punic Wars (264–146 BC), for which we aim to show the difference in panoplies, their modification and adaptations through the years of conflict.

*Contacts:*
E-mail: divulgacion.tanit@gmail.com
Facebook: https://www.facebook.com/TANITdivulgacion/?ref=page_internal

Legionaries advancing in line. (*Photo and copyright by Aera Legio I Consularis*)

## Insubria Gaesata

Insubria Gaesata is a cultural association based in Milan, Italy, which focuses on the historical re-enactment of the Celtic people that lived in the Northern part of Lombardy between the 3rd and 1st century BC. Through the constant and meticulous study and the collaboration with other experts and scholars we aim at reconstructing history, customs, religion, warfare and every aspect related to the Cisalpine and Alpine

Celts such as Insubri and Leponzi, but also the transalpine mercenaries known as Gaesati. Our main objective is spreading the interest in ancient history by taking part in historical re-enacment where we both expose the results of our studies with the aid of faithful reproductions of artifacts from the Iron Age, made by skilled artisans or by ourselves, and we pique the interest of the audience with the representation of battles and duels, always striving to recreate something as close as possible to the reality of the time. Our studies so far have been focused around the topics of warfare in the Celtic world, religion and rituality, medicine – enhanced by the use of natural remedies and plants – alimentation, writing and the material culture. All of this always making an effort by using a scientific and rigorous method, without ever falling into the suggestions offered by a certain revisionist milieu of the history of the Celtic period, influenced more by imaginative perceptions than by historical facts.

*Contacts:*
Facebook: https://www.facebook.com/InsubriaGaesata/

**Legio II Traiana Fortis – Cohors I Barcinonum, Barcino Oriens**

Barcino Oriens is a Roman historical re-enactment, reconstruction and disclosure group that was created in 2009, at the Joan Pelegrí School in Barcelona, to spread the knowledge of ancient Roman history so that everyone can see, feel and touch it. 'Seeing' means presenting activities that bring us closer to the reality of the ancient Roman world. 'Feeling' means showing each historical reconstruction in the closest way to the interlocutor so that he or she develops historical empathy. 'Touching' is making real the objects, images, tools, costumes and various aspects of antiquity to bring them closer to the viewer. The purpose of the recreation and historical reconstruction of Barcino Oriens is, therefore, to link and let people know, in a direct, attractive and emotional way, our awareness of our origins, the Roman Barcino. With Legio II Traiana Fortis – Cohors I Barcinonum we recreate and reconstruct different aspects of a Roman legion. You can learn what the panoply was like, how the legionaries were recruited and trained, how they lived in a *contubernium*, what the battle orders and instructions were, and much more. All historical reconstructions and re-enactments are accompanied by a rigorous historical and academic explanation about each of the aspects shown in classical Roman antiquity. We are educators of Roman history spreading Catalonia's archaeological heritage. All our performances are theatrical stagings of different aspects of life in ancient Rome, from the daily life of patrician ladies through to different aspects of military life: the way soldiers lived in a *contubernium*. It is a way of creating 'custom paintings' where these fragments of life are dramatized. All this is achieved through the performance of members of the group, who create characters that are part of each painting and explain the situation following a script that makes them interact with each other and with the audience. Each of the performances then becomes a small play (called a *pill*) that lasts between 30 and 45 minutes (depending on each historical re-enactment), where the situation presented to the audience is dramatized. We want the crowd to understand and participate in it, immersing them in the atmosphere and words of the characters, contemplating the materiel and costumes of our historical reconstruction. We want the audience to feel, live and touch the past through our representations, words and performances, and feel immersed in the world from 2,000 years ago. Ricard Llop Altés is the director of the group.

*Contacts:*
E-mail: barcinooriens@barcinooriens.cat
Website: www.barcinooriens.cat
Facebook: https://www.facebook.com/barcinooriens/

Legionaries in testudo defensive formation. (*Photo and copyright by Aera Legio I Consularis*)

## Legio VI Victrix Cohors II Cimbria

Legio VI Victrix Cohors II Cimbria is a Scandinavian Roman re-enactment group started in Denmark, today also with a chapter in Sweden and members from Germany as well. Our group consists of both military and civilian re-enactors. We re-enact the life in the Roman legions in the late first century AD and convey the life of the Roman Empire and its relations to the regions north of Germania Inferior, the Cimbrian peninsula and Scandia. Every summer Cohors II Cimbria participates in events both in Scandinavia and the rest of Europe. In the 'off-season' we research, lecture and are constantly developing our knowledge and equipment. Roman re-enactment is a never-ending process, as new archaeological finds and new theories keep appearing and constantly change the view of the Roman armies. Scandinavia was never a part of the Roman Empire, but due to our many bog findings, most of which are from the Roman period 0–350 AD, we have a lot of Roman artefacts in Scandinavia. Among these, the largest collection of Roman imperial weapons in the world outside Italy. The tribes that lived here at that time – mainly the Cimbrians, Teutons, Charudes and Sviones – were, from the time of Augustus and beyond, apparently on friendly terms with the Romans, or so the story goes. As you can read in the *Res Gestae of Augustus*, that primary source mentions an expedition to these most northern regions in year 5 AD led by Tiberius. That is one of many reasons why we find it proper to do Roman Re-enactment in Scandinavia. To us there is a forgotten story to be told.

*Contacts:*
E-mail: cohorsllcimbriadk@gmail.com
Website: https://cohorsllcimbria.com/
Facebook: https://www.facebook.com/Cohorsllcimbria/

## Legio XI C.P.F. Hispaniensis

Legio XI CPF Hispaniensis was created on 7 July 2018, founded by veteran Spanish and Swiss re-enactors who wanted to build an accurate historical re-enactment group in Spain. The group currently has twenty-five members and recreates Cohors III of Legio XI during the first century AD (Flavian times). The group is twinned with the Legio XI groups of Switzerland, Belgium and Russia. It is considered the best-dressed group in Europe and has participated in events such as Augusta Raurica and Natale di Roma, in addition to training and military ceremonies, marches and camps. Several of its members recreate Roman horsemen. All the group's activities are characterized by a high level of accuracy and professionalism.

Legionaries in testudo defensive formation. (*Photo and copyright by Aera Legio I Consularis*)

*Contacts:*
E-mail: cohorslemav@gmail.com
Facebook: https://www.facebook.com/LEGXICOHIII/

## Legio XIII Gemina

Legio XIII Gemina is an association dating back to 1992 and based in Vienna. The main focus is on the display of military life on the Danube border, with legionary as well as auxiliary soldiers, but we also try to recreate civilian life as accurately as possible. Our chosen time period is the turbulent years from the end of the reign of Emperor Nero up until Emperor Domitian. During the latter's reign, Legio XIII built the legionary fortress of Vindobona, modern-day Vienna. Our second military unit is Cohors II Italica Civium Romanorum, a rather interesting corps reconstructed according to a tombstone found at Carnuntum belonging to Proculus, an *Optio* of this cohort and also a member of a *vexillatio* of *sagittarii* (archers) of the army of Syria. This unit was probably sent to Pannonia during the civil wars of AD 69, the 'Year of the four Emperors'. Since our beginnings in the early years of Roman re-enactment, we have produced as much as possible of our equipment ourselves, staying in constant contact with museums and archaeologists for the latest scientific research, always trying to improve our gear and performances at public events. Our goal is to present a common Roman past, which stretches over wide parts of Europe and around the Mediterranean, to an interested public audience at events in Austria, Germany, Switzerland, Italy, France and the Czech Republic.

*Contacts:*
E-mail: obmann@legxiii.at
Website: http://www.legxiii.at
Facebook: https://www.facebook.com/Legio-XIII-Gemina-125111774228689

## Legio XIIII Gemina

Legio XIIII Gemina Martia Victrix is a re-enactment and living history group located in the United States, members of which are dedicated to representing the Roman legionary as he may have appeared during the years of the emperors from Nero to Trajan. We are a Roman re-enacting legion, with members from the United States and Canada, and our group is based out of Ohio and surrounding states. We strive for authenticity with our impressions to better educate the general public. Founded in 2015, our group seeks to recreate the equipment, routines and experiences of Roman legionaries from the first century AD for public, private and educational events.

*Contacts:*
E-mail: info@legxiiii.com
Website: http://legxiiii.com/
Facebook: https://www.facebook.com/legioxiiii/?ref=page_internal

## Lorica Romana

Lorica Romana (Legio X Gemina) is a historical reconstruction association that is based in the south of France near Nîmes (Nemausus). Our aim is to reproduce as faithfully as possible the Tenth Legion of the Roman Army from the time of Caesar until the end of the second century AD. This initial approach has been extended to other related fields of Roman antiquity. The presentation of civilian life, archers, Arecomic Volques auxiliaries and crafts allows us to get closer to other aspects of ancient civilization which left so many traces in our region. This approach is also accompanied by research in the context of archaeological experiments. These allow us to validate certain hypotheses and to stick as closely as possible to concrete reality. Apart from our services where an educational approach and exchanges with the public are at the heart of our concerns, we also produce documentary films in order to promote the revival of heritage sites that constitute our common history. Combining fun and education, we fully participate in this desire to bring history to life. Daniel Pirosa (Caivs Pirosvm Strabo) is the group's president, and Philippe Ciciarelli (Decimvs Vorenvs Madavros) its vice-president.

*Contacts:*
E-mail: loricaromana@outlook.fr
Website: www.loricaromana.fr
Facebook: https://www.facebook.com/LoricaRomana/

# Index